CW01091433

LIFE TO THE LEES

**A biography of Arthur Romney Green
furniture maker, boat builder
writer, teacher, poet, yachtsman,
social reformer, mathematician**

Susan Elkin

© Susan Elkin 1998
ISBN 1 897 887 13 2

Produced by Natula Publications.
5 St Margarets Avenue, Christchurch, Dorset. BH23 1JD

Printed by The Cromwell Press Ltd.
Trowbridge, Wiltshire.

A British Library Cataloguing-in-Publication Data.
A catalogue record for this book is available from the British Library.

Photographs on pages: 2, 6, 25, 56, 70 and 71 are author's own.

Illustrations on pages: 69, 129, 134, 136 are by kind permission of The Red House Museum, Christchurch

. . . I will drink
Life to the lees: all times I have enjoyed
Greatly . . .

Alfred Lord Tennyson, *Ulysses*.

Acknowledgements

I owe an enormous debt to Mike Allen of Christchurch and to John Whitehead of Newport. They have each given me more support and practical help than any biographer is entitled to hope for. Themselves both deeply interested in Green's life and work, Mike and John have both undertaken research and investigations and cheerfully shared their findings with me. They have also lent photographs from their private collections and allowed them to be reproduced here. It has been a great pleasure and privilege to get to know and to work with them.

Many thanks are also due to Dr Steven Yeo, grandson of W. Curtis Green and Romney Green's great-nephew. Steven has kindly given me access to family papers - along with friendly encouragement and his trust. The drawing of Bertha by Eric Gill is reproduced here, for the first time, by kind permission of Steven Yeo, as are the two anonymous sketches of Green and Bertha still in family possession.

I am grateful, too, to Graham Castle, John Champ and Alexander 'Sandy' Scott who worked in Romney Green's Bridge Street workshop in Christchurch. All three men have generously lent photographs for use in this book.

Philip Baker remembers as a child going into the workshop for lessons with Bertha Green; Captain A.E. Allen OBE RN lived nearby in Castle Street. They shared their memories happily with me, as did Mrs Kitty Prout who knew Green in Christchurch at the end of his life.

Kenneth Bowers of Saltburn met Romney Green at Chalfont and at Christchurch and was a personal friend of the Mather family. Mr A.E. Howarth of South London and Mr Arthur Grogan of Lewes contacted me with information on the whereabouts of several pieces of Green's furniture. I thank them all. I'm also grateful to Bert Wynn of Durham, an enthusiast, who sent me some fascinating photographs of his own work based on Green's designs and some up-to-date 'hands-on' information about construction.

Mary Greensted of Cheltenham Museums and Art Galleries; Jim Hunter of The Red House Museum in Christchurch; Sorrel Hershberg of the Department of Furniture and Woodwork at the Victoria and Albert Museum; Nicholas Rogers, archivist at Sidney Sussex College, Cambridge; Philippa Bassett, archivist (special collections) at The University of Birmingham; Alan Shrimpton, archivist at Bryanston School,

Dorset; the staff of the Local Studies Department of Surrey County Council Library Service and the staff at Christie's, King Street, London have all helped me in different ways for which I thank them most sincerely.

I'm obliged, too, to Dr Matthew Denney of Southampton University who generously shared part of his PhD research with me and to John and Fiona Breeze, friends who helped with information about the 'Kaffir War' of 1877/8.

I must also thank my elder son, Lucas Elkin and his wife Trudy. They have saved me many hours of work by tracking down, on my behalf, in Cambridge University Library, copies of articles by Green which were published in various journals and periodicals. My younger son, Felix Elkin, photographed Bertha Green's 'treasure box' and some other items for which I thank him.

Jane Martin of Natula Publications has been my editor and adviser as well as publisher. She has been a joy to work with. Without her *Life to the Lees* would never have come into fruition. She even undertook additional research and took some of the photographs herself.

But, most importantly of all, this book would certainly never have been written without the encouragement and sterling work of my meticulous, indefatigable husband, Nicholas Elkin, research assistant, proof reader and tea-maker extraordinaire. He has at every stage enthusiastically shared with me both the excitement and labour involved in this fascinating project: getting to know, and make better known, the compellingly charismatic Arthur Romney Green.

About the author

Susan Elkin, now an extensively published and prize-winning writer, was a full-time teacher of English in secondary schools for 25 years. In 1993 she resigned her post as Head of Upper School in a Kent school in order to develop further her writing career, already an increasingly demanding 'sideline'. She still teaches A level English in an independent school for a few hours per week in Kent, where she and her husband live.

She writes regularly on education matters for *The Sunday Times*, *Daily Mail*, *The Times* and other newspapers and magazines. She also writes widely on general interest topics and became interested in the history of woodwork, craft and its personalities through two substantial commissions - from *The Woodworker* and *Furniture and Cabinetmaking* - for series of articles on the 'descendants' of William Morris.

Susan has also written seven researched reports, published in book-form by Technology Colleges Trust, three self-help English books for home use by primary school children and an English Literature study guide. *Life to the Lees* is her first biography.

A chest made by Arthur Romney Green.

Contents

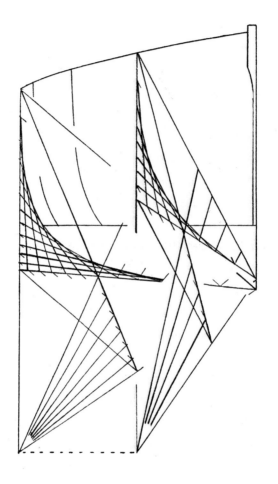

Letterhead of Arthur Romney Green. c. 1940

Illustrations

Illustrations (Continued)

Chapter 1 : Beginnings

When Arthur Romney Green was born on 16 February 1872, William Morris, whose example as an Arts and Crafts practitioner was eventually to influence him so profoundly, was 38. John Ruskin, whose writings were Green's lifelong inspiration was 53. And Queen Victoria was just over half way through her long reign.

Romney's birth took place at Wandsworth Common, London and he was the first child of Mr and Mrs Frederick Green. The new baby was named Arthur after his mother's much-loved brother, but his parents and other members of the family always used his middle name, Romney, whose 'o" is pronounced as a short 'u' as in 'rum'.

Fred, as he was usually known, was a barrister whose comfortably-placed Quaker family came from Saffron Walden in Essex. Maria Heath Green, known as Minnie, was a member of the well known Curtis family, many of them doctors, who had lived and practised in the family home on Normandy Hill in Alton, Hampshire for eight generations.

The Greens had met through Fred's older brother, Henry, who answered an advertisement in *The Friend*, a Quaker newspaper, placed by Minnie's father, Dr William Curtis. Henry Green's two year stint as an articled pupil in the dispensary at Alton led to his family and his employer's family getting to know each other.

Ten months before the birth of their first child Minnie and Fred were married, like so many of Minnie's Curtis ancestors, at the old Friends Meeting House in Alton. Their wedding day 'was a typical April day of sunshine and showers,' wrote Minnie in old age, going on to reflect that the rest of their short, twelve year marriage was like that too, although with characteristic cheerfulness she also observed that most of the clouds were 'silver lined'.

At first, however, from their lovely honeymoon in Devon onwards, all went well. Their new house, 2 Kingsdown Villas, Bolingbroke Grove, is at the northern corner of Wandsworth Common, London SW11. Solidly built and semi-detached with four storeys, it was a typical new Victorian 'villa', with bow windows at the front, built at the same time as the streets of Wandsworth and Battersea that you see today were being developed from formerly open fields. The house the Green family lived in, now subdivided for multi-occupation, overlooks the Common where, in the 1870s, cows grazed among the elm and poplar trees.

2 Kingsdown Villas, Bolingbroke Grove, Wandsworth.

When he was about six weeks old Minnie took her new baby to Alton for a visit to his maternal grandparents, the first of many happy times Romney would spend in that old house which had seen so many generations of Curtises. He spent his first Christmas with his other grandparents at Saffron Walden. He was to enjoy many happy childhood holidays there too amongst the cattle, wild flowers and good food which Mr and Mrs Green senior had in abundance.

The Green family lived at Wandsworth for six years. Fred Green, with all the habits and tastes of an English gentleman, commuted daily, either by horsedrawn bus, Hansom cab or by suburban train to his London chambers. Minnie, assisted by at least two maids, cared for her children. Margaret in 1874 and William in 1875, soon arrived. In the family the children were known by the pet names of Vonny, Daisy and Poppo respectively.

Fred Green was academically able and had taken an MA at The University of London before opting for the Bar. He had style too. A dark, striking looking man with olive skin and strong features, he wore his hair brushed upwards away from his forehead like a sooty halo. The smart rapier walking-stick which he often carried was much envied by both his young sons. Green senior had a beautiful speaking voice and sometimes gave lectures. And, quite glamorously, he had distinguished himself at age 17 by being the youngest Englishman to have climbed Mont Blanc.

He had been an enthusiastic naturalist from boyhood and a great shot, although he taught his sons not to shoot anything which they didn't intend to eat. His extensive collection of butterflies was stored in a splendid Victorian cabinet of 30 drawers - in which, decades later, Green was to store designs and manuscripts at Christchurch.

Green later recalled his father as a 'playful disciplinarian' who left to his wife the serious business of teaching the children what was what. Fred had grown up with horses so, having rigorously tutored his wife in horse riding before they were married, he taught his children to ride, on hired ponies, as soon as they were old enough.

According to his elder son the father wasn't quite the saint his wife believed him to be and occasionally behaved 'badly'. Once, for example, he beat Romney's little brother William with an umbrella because the child had fallen over on the mud. Another time he deliberately took horses and children to wait beneath a railway bridge to enjoy the fun of their being startled by a train thundering overhead. Fortunately no train came.

Fred Green's politics were passionately Liberal and he was summed up by his son later in life as 'a good man according to his lights,' although Romney doubted, perhaps unfairly, that either of his parents knew anything at all of the struggles and maltreatment of factory workers or agricultural labourers in the 1870s. Later, Romney Green, the social reformer, believed that it was he who had educated his mother about the plight of those he habitually referred to as 'bottom dogs'.

Romney's father had a talent for making friends with attractive women who then became part of the family circle of friends, long after Fred's death. The sister-in-law of Dr Cock, the family doctor, was one of these. Mrs Willoughby Hodgson would call on the Green family on Sunday evenings to play and sing with the adults and to help the children with their singing, dancing and recitation.

Bolingbroke Grove, Wandsworth Common c. 1900.

Another family friend was the second wife of the Solicitor General to the Post Office, Sir Robert Hunter, with whom Frederick Green had been at university. Hunter and his first wife - who died in childbirth a few weeks before Romney was born - were near neighbours in Wandsworth. Eventually Hunter and his second wife settled in Haslemere in Surrey where the Greens spent many memorable childhood holidays. The Hunters were instrumental twenty years later in Romney Green's decision to set up a workshop at Haslemere.

Several things happened to Romney Green when he was about five. His parents were gradually drawn away from their ancestral Quakerism towards the Church of England. This came about partly because they were influenced by the writings of F.D. Maurice, whom they had also heard preach in London. Fred Green also believed that fellowship was a vital part of religion but there were few Quakers amongst his London circle. Both he and his wife were deeply committed Christians - and it wasn't without a great deal of thought and prayer that they finally converted from Quakerism. On 25th July 1878 they were baptised just round the corner from their Wandsworth home by Canon Erskine Clarke at the newly-built St Mark's Church with its colourful brick patterning. The children were baptised a week or so later.

Apart from having them baptised, Minnie Green never imposed her profound religious convictions on her children as they grew up, trusting that they would one day find their own way to faith. As Romney remarked many years later, she was almost right. Her two younger children and all her grandchildren became, and remained, convinced believers. Only Romney dissented. His 'religious' beliefs in adult life were consistently flexible and rather more metaphysical than orthodox. He never really regarded himself as a committed Christian and he was not a regular churchgoer.

'Vonny' was described in letters to and from his grandparents as a good and happy little boy. He loved being read to and showed an intelligent interest in what went on around him. His mother, who was quite practical, and his father who dabbled with a little amateur carpentry, began to show him how to make things. It was when his son was about five that Fred recorded in a letter that Romney had begun to make suites of furniture out of paper.

It was also in 1877 that Fred Green's illness - the tuberculosis which was to kill him six years later - first began to show as a serious problem. He had a cough and a series of throat infections. Then, alarmingly, his doctors confirmed that the lungs were also infected. A spell in a warm climate was recommended.

Reluctantly leaving Margaret and William with their Alton grandparents, Fred and Minnie Green decided to leave the smoggy damp of London and try a spell in the warm and 'healthy' climate of South Africa. Because of Romney's tendency to asthma and recurrent bronchitis they took their elder son with them. From then on the family were, in part, dependant upon the Green grandparents at Saffron Walden, and on other relations, for financial support. Mr and Mrs Green senior, for example, sold their coach and pair in order to help their son in his illness.

St Mark's Church, Battersea.

The young couple and their small son sailed from Southampton on *The Nubian*, a ship owned by R.U.S.S. Co., on 11th October 1877. It was a rotten journey south via Madeira. Minnie was very seasick and Romney spent much of the journey in his bunk. When they finally arrived in Cape Town on 4th November Minnie and Fred were entranced by the sight of Table Mountain at dusk and their first glimpse of the Southern Cross. His mother recorded her sadness that Romney was asleep and missed these sights.

The Greens remained in South Africa for just six months. The trip was not a success. First there was a war. Throughout the nineteenth century the Xhosa branch of the Bantu people, then known as 'Kaffirs', were in intermittent conflict with the white settlers in the eastern frontier region. In late 1877 and early 1878 hostilities intensified because, by then, most of the aggrieved tribesman were armed with European firearms. It was not a comfortable time for a British family to arrive in the colony.

Secondly, severe drought meant that the food available was very poor and it certainly didn't do much to help a sick man to recover. Butter and

6

milk were great luxuries for example. And the circuit for a barrister was very demanding. 'You need to be strong and to have money to survive as a barrister in South Africa,' Minnie observed ruefully.

Nonetheless, as a man of the law, Fred enjoyed a certain amount of prestige and generally found that he was sought out by interesting and well-connected people such as the clergy and the local lawyers. Before they left there Minnie had to make dozens of calls and she wrote to friends in South Africa for many years afterwards.

For most of their time in South Africa the Greens lodged in a low Dutch boarding house called 'Roseneath' at Grahamstown, having made the long 70 mile journey to it in a bumpy ox-cart from Port Elizabeth. It took five hours and it was difficult for Minnie with a sick husband and a tired and delicate child. Then they waited six weeks for their luggage to reach them.

The five-year old Romney Green remembered for ever the hills with their red aloes, which are birds similar to humming birds but slightly larger. Neither did he forget the huge vultures which occasionally swooped down to feed on beasts which had died of thirst by the roadside.

Fred, of course, was captivated by the wonderful South African butterflies, birds and locusts and began to teach his elder son the art of collecting them. For the rest of his life, like his father before him, Romney was thrilled at the sight of a clouded yellow, a fritillary or even a peacock butterfly.

Minnie shared the butterfly hobby and took her son for long walks. She also made some attractive sketches of South African wildlife and scenery, some of which Romney kept and still had at the end of his life. Like several of her Curtis forbears - and like her daughter Margaret, who went on to exhibit at The Royal Academy - Minnie Green was an accomplished artist. The Curtis Museum in Alton has several examples of drawings and paintings by her aunts and great aunts.

23rd May 1878 found the Green family heading thankfully, but also a little shame-facedly, for home, once more aboard *The Nubian*. They reached Southampton on 21st June and were overjoyed to be reunited with their two younger children and with the rest of the family.

By the Christmas of that year they were installed in a cottage at Lympstone, north east of Exmouth on the Exe estuary, having looked around and chosen Devon as being a likely place for a consumptive man to recover. Fred, however, was too ill to work every day, although the sea air was thought to be much healthier for a consumptive man than the smoke-laden atmosphere of London.

They ate good food and, in a delightful glimpse of family life, Minnie describes the children sitting up at teatime joking with Fred. They all called each other silly names, aided and abetted by their father. Romney invariably laughed long and loud on these occasions - for the rest of his life people would comment on the spontaneous naturalness of his engaging laugh.

After six months in Lympstone the family settled in Exmouth. From here Fred could travel to chambers in Exeter once a week - as his health gradually declined.

At about this time Minnie Green, an excellent teacher, set about the more formal education of her children. She taught them all the elementary subjects each morning. In the afternoons Romney's father grounded him in the basics of Latin and French. Romney was a thoughtful child, often asking his parents searching questions such as, with unconscious echoes of the doomed Macduff child in *Macbeth*, 'Is my father a good man?' Romney was little more than a toddler when his mother, laughing at her son's naive perspicacity, struggled to answer this one.

Thoughtfulness often manifested itself as endearing absent-mindedness, a quality which he retained for the rest of his life, and which his only daughter, Beatrice, inherited in large measure according to the family descendants who remember her. Green, laughing in great gales as was his wont, used to tell against himself the story of how, as a boy, he was once asked to pour out a dose of medicine for his mother. This he did. Then, without thinking, he drank it himself. In adult life there was a famous occasion when, on his way from Christchurch to Oxford by train, he became so engrossed in the writing of a long poem that he ended up in London - having not noticed the names of the stations he had passed through.

When he was nine Romney Green started as a day boy at a small 'prep' school, St Peter's, in Exmouth. The two head boys there were fourteen years old and Romney - very competitive at that stage - tried hard to beat them at their school work. He didn't. But, at the end of his first year and just a few months before his father's death, he managed to secure a special prize for coming second in both mathematics and classics. His efforts were evidently recognised by the teaching staff.

The 10-year old Green also beat the 14-year old school chess champion by 'hooking his queen'. Chess was to be one of Green's life-long passions. He first learnt it from an eccentric, white-bearded, septuagenarian friend of his father's. Mr Kennedy, founder of the Alpine Club - 'prime hero of my youth' - also coached him in algebra during the school holidays and taught him to skate and to swim, spartanly insisting that the latter activity should take place every day regardless of season, before breakfast, naked and without the use of a towel.

Fred Green died, after a long struggle, on 9th December 1883, just a few weeks before his elder son's eleventh birthday. He was 38 years old.

Minnie was left with very little money and three young children aged 10, 8 and 7. Thereafter she and her family were dependent on financial help from relatives and friends. Her husband had been ailing drastically for more than a year and the whole family understood that he was dying. Green said later that he believed that his father knew he hadn't long to live from their first settling at Exmouth.

'Be noble, be good, be true' were the dying man's last words to his children. 'I think I have been fairly good and true,' wrote Romney half a century later, 'but the epithet "noble", which he himself [Fred Green] so richly deserved, is not for me.'

Romney Green was 13, and still at prep school, when he built his first little flat-bottomed skiff or 'sharpie', thus embarking on another life-long love affair - with boats and boat building. Completely untrained in boat building, he worked out his own constructional method by making the sides from match boarding placed vertically. It proved surprisingly strong and Green and a friend had a lot of fun sailing her amongst the waves and breakers between Coombe Point and Exmouth.

Armed with a single-barrel muzzle-loading gun given him by a sporting uncle, he also shot a few birds in the Exe estuary, insisting as his father had taught him, that all game be eaten - even down to a brace of guillemots. In those far off days of innocence and freedom, when parents felt they could allow their offspring licence to discover the world without worrying overtly about danger, his mother encouraged all this outdoor activity and fresh air, believing that it would be good for his weak chest.

He made a second boat when he was 15, once again innovatively working out the practicalities for himself.

'She was about 16' by 4'3", flat-bottomed, but not straight-bottomed,' he wrote nostalgically many years later. 'I knew my limitation as a craftsman too well to attempt fitting her with a centreboard case, but I had enough mechanical sense to see that a keel 8"or 9" deep, though it was only made of 1" deal, would stand up to its work on her rockered bottom, as it would not do on a straight-bottomed duck punt, and that it would strengthen the boat. I fitted this and can recommend the idea, which I do not think has been otherwise tried, to boy boat builders.'

He called her *The Argo*. Together Romney and *The Argo* explored the coast between Dartmouth and Exmouth sailing single-handedly. He often slept 'away', catching and cooking mackerel to eat. Inspired as he would be for the rest of his life by the quiet, self-sufficiency and freedom of cruising, he wrote poetry when he was moored for the night.

At about the same time as he built *The Argo* Green changed schools, progressing to Newton College, a Quaker boarding school inland at Newton Abbot and to which he won a small scholarship. The balance of his fees were paid by a relative of his mother.

He was lonely at first. He missed his boat and he missed the sea, often climbing the hills on his own on a Sunday afternoon to catch a glimpse of the coast. It was butterflies, his father's old love, which rescued him.

The headmaster, G. Townsend-Warner, must have been a perceptive and sensitive man. Noticing Green's unhappiness and discovering that he was a butterfly collector, Townsend-Warner allowed the boy freedom to roam, explore and collect at weekends, on half-holidays and sometimes at night. He, and another boy, Jack Comyns, were often excused Saturday games and tea so that they could fit in long walks. Often the two boys treated themselves to a 'wonderful tea' in Bovey Tracey on the way back. Many years later Green, who always appreciated good food, recorded his memory of those 'boiled eggs, bread and butter and cake and jam, strawberries and enormous bowls of Devonshire cream, at one shilling [5p] per head.'

During some of these walks Green introduced Comyns to the delights of the English poets. He had, by now, been reading eclectically for many years. Minnie was, and Fred had been, great readers of poetry, fiction, history, biography, theology, philosophy and social history. They were also both knowledgeable and accomplished in literary matters. Each of them lengthily wrote down their thoughts in letters, journals and memoirs. Quite unassumingly much of this *modus vivendi* was passed to their children. Green was to be a compulsive 'scribbler' on many subjects for the rest of his life and had been penning poems from infancy.

Green played cricket and Rugby at Newton College and quite enjoyed them, although the only sport he liked watching was first-class tennis.

What to do upon leaving school? The uncle who had paid for his school fees offered to find Romney a position in his office. That didn't appeal. Minnie Green wanted him to go into the Church.

What the boy would really have liked was to earn his living as a boat builder or as a poet, and although he was to build boats and write poems for the rest of his life, he knew, even as a teenager, that he was unlikely to be able to keep himself by doing either. And he was, evidently, going to have to aim for self-sufficiency because, as he put it, 'I knew that my widowed mother was as poor as a church mouse.' Oddly, he was doubtful even at that stage that he had the personality ever to earn a decent living.

The uncle, with an eye on a career in the Church for his nephew, offered to fund the boy through university. If Romney could secure some kind of scholarship then his uncle would make up the difference. Not knowing what he should specialise in Romney sought advice from Mr Kennedy. 'Take mathematics,' the old man said, 'it is the key to all sciences and will enable you to learn any other subject you require in just six weeks.'

The trouble was that Romney, by his own admission, was not very good at mathematics. But he manfully tried to study it on his own in order to sit the Cambridge University Scholarship papers in the subject.

By then, however, like many adolescent boys before and since, he had already discovered the joys of female company. He was rapidly developing into a fine looking man with a straight back and strong features. His mouth was full and sensual and his eyes were a piercing blue. It's a pity that Green's life predated colour photography but several of those still living who knew him remember those eyes.

His unusually direct way of looking at people seems to have been part of his life-long ability to sweep people along. His friends, family and employees mostly liked and, often adored him so that they usually did what he wanted, forgiving him his 'wrongs' quite readily.

He had a distinctly pleasing manner. Women were almost always to find him charismatically attractive for the rest of his life. At 17 he was distracted from his studies by romantic urges to read poetry and novels instead of maths. On the first day of his exam he was stunned to receive a, hopelessly impractical, written proposal of marriage from a girl named Cynthia - with whom he had for some time been conducting a chaste, but passionate, liaison - mostly from afar.

He was also simultaneously enamoured of a young girl who was vibrant, playful and attractive. Her brothers and the Green boys were friendly.

Romney dubs her 'Stella' in his autobiography because, at the time of his writing, she was still alive. In time, after he had left school, the relationship with Stella became his first fully-developed sexual one.

His attitude to sex was sacramental. He regarded it as an outward and visible sign of something inward and almost spiritual. He always enjoyed the company of women and the pleasure which their bodies could give him, but he seems never to have seen women merely as objects. Rather, he habitually regarded sex as something too special to be dismissed lightly or frivolously. Sex was a subject in which he showed a lively life-long interest and about which he was surprisingly candid. He was almost never without some sort of sexual partner: girl friend, wife or mistress, from his teens to his death. His need for physical sex was evidently powerful, although deliberately and carefully controlled.

Meanwhile, Green was astonished to be awarded a small open exhibition worth £3 per year at Sidney Sussex College. He went up to Cambridge in the autumn of 1891 and was quickly proved right: his mathematical talents were indeed modest. He claimed afterwards not to have understood a word of the lectures and to have known very early on in his course that he would certainly not achieve a first-class degree.

He later insisted that he learned very little maths at Cambridge. But he made some good friends, one of whom was G.P. Gooch, the historian, who later generously helped Green financially. He read a lot of books, reflected at length, grew up a good deal and realised early on that, however much it might disappoint his mother, he couldn't possibly become a clergyman. He rowed in the Sidney Sussex eight and won the Maiden Sculls in his first term. He was a good weight for a rower: Sidney Sussex's archives show that he tipped the scales at just over 11 stone throughout his Cambridge days.

He commented later that 'in a small college if you row and play rugby you must sometimes row a trial eight race in the morning and play a football match in the afternoon, with an intervening lunch of beefsteak and champagne - such was the prescription. And so the time passed merrily away.'

In the event, his preoccupation with 'Stella' and with a new love cost him even a second-class degree and he graduated with a third in the summer of 1894. He was 22 years old.

Chapter 2: Teaching, Marriage and Durban

At this point Green decided that there was nothing for it; he would have to become a school master. He'd found much of the teaching served up to him as a pupil and an undergraduate, narrowly dull - and some if it incomprehensible. By his own admission he was academically indifferent. Nonetheless, like many teachers before him and since, he drifted into the profession because he could think of nothing else to do. As George Bernard Shaw wrote in his essay 'Education': 'He who can, does. He who cannot, teaches.'

Yet, it was an interesting decision in Green's case because he was to remain a teacher or instructor, and by all accounts eventually a good one, on and off for most of the rest of his life. Teaching and learning became yet another of his life themes. He came to develop quite forward-thinking ideas about what children - and adults - should learn and how they should learn it. He only came to appreciate the value of his own grounding in mathematics for example, when he discovered its usefulness as a design method for furniture and boats.

Dismissive of the dull limitations of the 'pure' maths he had mostly been obliged to study at school and at Cambridge, he developed the view that children would learn far more effectively and readily if they were led to see a practical and joyful purpose in what they were doing. And if any 'Serious Mathematician' accused him of Philistinism, Green would counter by saying that fishermen probably see their fish as an enjoyable end in itself but they don't bring home inedible fish. Or, that amateur sailors love their hobby for itself - but they still like to pretend that they're going somewhere.

The 1890s saw the opening of the earliest technical schools and Green thought that he might be better suited to teach in one of these than in what he called an 'ordinary boys' school', by which he meant the sort of fee-paying establishment that he had attended himself. He also remarked with uncharacteristic bitterness that he suspected that his third-class degree would probably open the door to only a third-class job. In the autumn of 1894 he therefore enrolled at Mason College, Birmingham (now part of The University of Birmingham) on a general course in chemistry for two terms at a cost of £5-5-0 (£5.25). He also paid an additional £1-11-6 (£1.58) for six hours use of the physics laboratory during the academic year 1894/95. He stated his intended profession, upon enrolment, as teaching.

In the 1895/96 and 1896/97 academic years at Mason College, Green took courses only in physics. During the final year he obtained a full concession on his course fees by working as a 'demonstrator in physics'. He also helped to keep himself, so that he could give his mother something towards housekeeping costs, by teaching some evening sessions at local technical schools and one class on perspective drawing at the school of art.

Minnie had moved the family from Exmouth to 1 Thynne Street, Christ Church in West Bromwich by now, so Green was able to live at 'home'. The move to the Midlands had come about because Margaret, Romney's younger sister, was showing artistic talent and had been offered a place at West Bromwich Art School where a family friend, Joseph Pearce, was the principal.

William Green, Romney's younger brother, had not flourished at Newton College and had left early. A decision was made that he too might try his luck at the art school. There he blossomed and left two years later to take a job, with prospects, in London and through which he rose eventually to become the famous and award-winning architect, William Curtis Green RA, achieving infinitely more fame, prosperity and respectability than his elder brother. As Romney, the teacher, later commented, 'Newton College was a good school but the ineffectiveness of the school curriculum in developing the latent faculty of the school boy is thus plainly exposed.'

Before leaving Cambridge and taking his finals he had met an alluring young woman, a fair-haired beauty, named Florence Emma Garman, almost certainly familiarly known as 'Flossie' or 'Florrie'. She was the eldest of four sisters and Green was introduced to her because his sister and Florence's sisters had become friends at West Bromwich Art School. The daughter of a stylish surgeon and country doctor, William Chancellor Garman, Florence also had three dashing brothers, at least one of whom followed his father into the medical profession.

The whole Garman family were, in Green's words: 'rather fast, horsy, jolly, tennis-playing people.' They lived in style at Yew Tree House at the village of Great Barr, then in Staffordshire, not far from West Bromwich. They were also well versed in literature and music and were witty and entertaining with words. Green found all the Garmans very attractive, especially Florence who was seven years his senior. Soon he was hopelessly in love with her. And 'Stella' - who had been with him as recently as at the May races in Cambridge earlier in 1894 - was cast aside, although not without some sadness.

14

Florence took the initiative. She was 'very far from fiercely pure' and 'generous with what her brothers had taught her.' Green didn't feel ashamed or especially responsible, as he had done in earlier relationships, because he reasoned that, being older, she knew what she was doing. Soon they were engaged and her father was furious. His misgivings about Romney Green were perfectly understandable. Dr Garman didn't want for his eldest daughter a fatherless, penniless young man who appeared to be a 'perpetual student', without any prospect of getting a good degree (in fact, according to Mason College archives, Green failed to graduate after more than two years full-time there) or of obtaining any kind of proper job.

Florence's wise and kindly siblings tried hard to warn Green off the marriage for his own sake. They told him that Florence was an incorrigible flirt with expensive tastes and would never settle and be happy for long with a poor man. They also counselled their angry father to invite Green to the house and let the young man see Florence in her true colours. That, they argued, would soon disillusion Green.

But it wasn't to be. The father forbade them to meet - so they set up clandestine trysts. Green summed it up: 'A romantic series of stolen interviews sealed my fate.' She introduced him to the poetry of Ralph Waldo Emerson and he wrote passionate love poetry to her - as he did to every woman he was enamoured of - as well as a longish poem based on Goethe's *Fredericka* which was published in Lawrence Binyon's anthology *The Garland*.

> Daughter, my wife of some patrician house
> When I those large and soft blue eyes behold,

> Those sweetly arched, finely pencilled brows
> That hair thy crown, of immaterial gold -

begins his poem 'To My Wife'.

Then, having given up his course at Mason College and having failed to be appointed to the staff of a technical school in Kent, Green accepted a teaching job in South Africa. Durban Government High School - a day school - offered him the post of senior mathematical and science master with a salary sufficient to support a wife.

Dr Garman, Florence's father, then gave in and agreed to their marriage, to Minnie Green's horror. It was a double wedding on 28th April 1897, with

Florence's elder brother Walter and his bride. Green, whose profession is given on the marriage certificate as 'tutor', and Florence were married by Rev. Charles Bodington in the village church at Great Barr. They had travelled there in a postillion given by Florence's otherwise miserly father. The only other thing the old man did for his daughter, Green records crossly, was to agree to continue to pay her 'beggarly dress allowance of £20 per year.'

A week's honeymoon in Cannock Chase followed. She was young for her age and keen to make love frequently. Green - with rather surprising Puritanism - believed, like Socrates, that sex is best enjoyed sparingly. He also harboured a curious Victorian belief that too much sex is bad for your health, after the teachings of Herbert Spencer and Dr Plummer. Presumably - although he was to modify his views later - he reached these conclusions at this stage of his life because now, for the first time, he could indulge in sex freely and as often as he wanted. Of course his abstemious and self-denying attitude made problems for his 'generous' wife. This friction made her a less 'docile and sympathetic mate than she might have been' and he later regretted his failure to enjoy her 'great gift' as fully as he might have done.

Florence always claimed to be 'modern' and 'progressive', insisting that both she and Green would always be 'free'. This seems to have meant in practice that she reserved for herself the right to 'flirt'. And in a half-jocular way she encouraged her husband to do likewise, but the frivolity of flirting was never really his way. Besides, for several years he remained so much in love with Florence that he was impervious to the charms of any other woman.

Immediately after the honeymoon the newlyweds, Mr and Mrs Romney Green, set sail for South Africa - which must surely have brought back memories for him of 1877 and his voyage on *The Nubian* twenty years earlier. This time the journey was much pleasanter. The three-week voyage took place on a small cargo boat, passage paid by the Natal Government. There were only about 12 passengers. Romney and Florence enjoyed each other's company. She was a relaxed companion and both of them made friends quite easily. Green taught the first mate the mathematical principles of navigation and, in return, he taught Green the practical side of it. The two men had some excellent games of chess too. It was an enjoyable trip during which neither Romney nor Florence suffered from much sea-sickness.

On arrival in Durban they were both impressed by what Green recalled as 'the great stalls of sub-tropical fruit, the rickshaw boys with their polished black limbs, red-bound holland jerkins and various head-dresses.' They were taken by one-horse tram up to The Berea, an area of high ground outside the city, where the school stood beneath long rows of red-flowering trees.

He was romantically inclined to the South African atmosphere and climate. Green's poem 'Natal: An Ode' includes the passage:

> . . . Fair Land, the odour and the bloom,
> Each aromatic shrub and flowering tree
> With those sweet name we shall remember thee;
> Fields of bananas, sugar, maize and pine;
> Groves where the orange and lemon shine
> Like stars out of their shadowy firmament;
> Those feathery cusps of scarlet flower that plume
> The leafless grey stems of the kafir boom;
> The prickly cactus; the delicious scent
> Of the great blue-gums; the perpetual sigh
> Of ocean rising in our wreathed balcony;

Green and his wife were assigned to an old bungalow in a grove of orange and lemon trees (to which he refers in 'Natal: An Ode') about ten minutes' walk down the slope from the school. They enjoyed settling themselves in. Green felt that they could manage by themselves for a while, but Florence - true to her sisters' prediction that she would never make a poor man's wife - lost no time in recruiting resident domestic help: two true-bred Zulu boys.

This casually superior attitude was what Green, the developing socialist, regarded as the 'Tory' in Florence and it was to cause friction. Notwithstanding the fact that his mother had always had help in the house while her children were growing up, Green greatly admired those who did their own 'housework'.

Nontheless Green recalled the two boys he was persuaded to employ, as being great fun. He and his friends would chase them in play which made the boys shriek with laughter. Both would run barefoot at full speed over a newly made road, but on Sundays they manfully forced themselves into top hats and boots which made them hobble about like old men. One of them, Charlie, was taken ill at one point and his father, a magnificent looking Zulu chief and medicine man, moved into the Greens' bungalow for three days until the boy had recovered.

Two young bachelor teaching colleagues, fair-haired Bangley and dark-haired Garrod, rented the stables attached to the Greens' bungalow.

17

Bangley, in flight from a love affair which had gone awry in England, taught classics and occasionally stood in for the headmaster. Both owned ponies. The rent they paid was sufficient to meet the wages of the Greens' second house boy. Bangley and Garrod were frequent visitors to the Greens and joined in the horseplay with the servant boys.

Green claimed later that he hated the work in South Africa, although his pupils did reasonably well in academic terms. He successfully coached two candidates for the Natal scholarship at Cambridge and his School Certificate results were satisfactory. He didn't regard himself as a natural teacher and, like Charlotte Brontë's Lucy Snow or D.H. Lawrence's Ursula Brangwen, he found the discipline difficult, especially without the sympathetic support of the headmaster. For a man so thoughtful and humane it is surprising, and rather sad, to find him commenting that any teacher must be 'ready to resort to violence at a moment's notice' and pointing out that 'schoolboys must always be treated as potential enemies rather than as human beings.'

He describes a telling Durban incident which doesn't, to modern eyes, show him in a good light on several counts. Someone had released a large insect in the aisle in the classroom. Green identified the culprit whom he dismissed cuttingly as 'a lusty little Boer Jew of 15.' Green promptly seized 'that little devil', inverted him across his knee and spanked the boy with his bare hand until he howled.

But out of school hours he thoroughly enjoyed himself. He and Florence used a generous wedding present from his old university friend Gooch to buy a 'sociable bicycle' which they had brought from Britain. It was better than a tandem for newly-weds or lovers because the riders sat side-by-side rather than one behind the other. They used it for shopping in Durban and for visiting friends on The Berea.

With the £20 of Gooch's gift that was left over, Green started to build his third boat. It took him six months to produce a sailing canoe with a heavy plate 18' by 4'6" of pentagonal cross-section, in the American style. The practical Minnie, back in England, recast some of the metal work which he had used in his very first boat more than ten years earlier and sent it out. By 1898 he and Florence, sometimes accompanied by some of their friends, were able to embark on regular sailing excursions in Durban Bay. It was eight miles long by two wide, with an attractive island on which they often picnicked.

They enjoyed several good holidays on an up-country stock farm where they hired ponies and stayed 'all-found' for 2/6d (12p) per week. He was occasionally invited to shoot with friends too. Green wrote an article for

Yachting Monthly about Captain Slocum who passed through Durban on his boat *The Spray* during his time there. Green also did some (paid) pieces for the *Natal Mercury*.

Unlike Minnie Green a generation earlier, Florence did not conceive a baby within weeks of marriage. Green professed an abhorrence for mechanical contraception - discovering many years later in conversation with his mother that this point of view he would have shared with Fred, his father - so non-conception is unlikely to have been deliberate. Green did however later admit that at times when, for whatever reason, babies were best avoided he preferred to refrain from love-making other than during the 'safe-period'. Florence, moreover, underwent some painful medical treatment for 'a trouble which delayed the birth of our daughter' while they were in Durban.

As a childless wife with few domestic responsibilities, she found time to flirt with the headmaster - who responded well to someone who would stand up to him with 'cheek'. She also flirted more seriously with a local man, a Scottish banker who was quite well off. Many years later, after Green had left her and after she had divorced him, Florence came close to marrying this old flame from Durban days. For now, as usual, she casually amused herself by trying, half-playfully, to persuade the reluctant Green to embark on some amicable flirtations of his own with her women friends.

Then Florence developed mild asthma and Green saw more of her inability to make a success of being a poor man's wife. Having been recommended by her doctor to move to a higher and more open site she wanted to move house. Green had received a small legacy from a Curtis relative so, on the advice of his wife's banker friend, he agreed to buy, on mortgage, a plot of land further up the Berea ridge. It had a splendid sea view and was nearer to the school. Because he was beginning to read Ruskin and to dabble in design construction, Green thought it would be fun to design and personally supervise the building of the house - which he did. He made several pieces of furniture too. Six months later they moved in.

Living expenses, however, were beginning to escalate. Green's salary simply wouldn't finance the lifestyle which Florence wanted. The grocery bill alone, he records ruefully, took more than half his monthly salary. Florence's sister, Mary, came to Natal for an extended holiday and was soon entertaining her admirers as well as Florence's. And it was all at Green's expense. Inevitably it created tension, although Green insisted that he still loved Florence too much at this time for there to be any serious quarrelling.

Examples of furniture made by Arthur Romney Green.

It wasn't just the cost of it all that irked him either. Green was temperamentally fairly abstemious. He had built his boat and had bought a set of Encyclopaedia Britannica when his legacy first arrived. He wanted for nothing else. He simply didn't like 'luxury' very much, associating it perhaps with what he perceived as 'Tory' ostentatiousness about wealth - which he disliked acutely.

'I merely knew that the world contained a lot of poor people, and I thought that luxury should be barred in all classes until this ceased to be the case. I had been used to the good plain meals of my mother's economical housekeeping and I disliked, even apart from the expense, what I regarded as the luxury of my wife's table', he wrote.

Then one day Garrod made a chance remark which was to change the course of Green's life. He looked at the boat and at the furniture which Green had made for his Durban home and said: 'If I could do work like that I'd give up this business of schoolmastering and set up as a gentleman woodworker.' And that, after the outbreak of the Boer War in 1899, and following the end of Green's three-year contract in Durban, was exactly what he did in mid-1900.

Chapter 3: A Workshop in Sussex

Green considered setting up a workshop in Durban in partnership with the Scotsman who had built his house there. But it fell through. He was feeling mildly homesick and his mother was keen to have her firstborn and his wife back in England. So Florence's sister, who was about to be married in Natal and Bangley, between them, sold the house on Durban's Berea which Green and Florence had built and bought. The Greens set sail for Britain and arrived a few months into the new century.

Romney's younger sister Margaret, who was shortly to marry a Curtis cousin and was beginning to make her way as a water-colourist, had found a former rectory called 'Critchfield' at Bosham in Sussex, which Green rented, furnished, for £20 per year. Now a bed and breakfast establishment, Critchfield is an attractive, red brick 18th, or early 19th, century house which sits at right angles to the road in quite a large garden.

'Happy Bosham' as he called it, is a delightfully pretty village in a corner of Chichester Harbour. The sea washes twice-daily over the harbour road at high tide and the boats bob within a few yards of the buildings. It was an ideal place for a man to whom boats meant so much. Almost every home he had from birth to death was within striking distance of water to sail on and swim in.

Green converted Critchfield's stables into a workshop and began by making some simple furniture for his sister. It was a real family effort because Green's brother William, who had married Cicely Dilkes in 1899, contributed the designs. In retrospect, Green acknowledged that constructing to his brother's designs helped him to develop both manufacturing techniques and designs of his own.

For a while Green worked alone and then, in time, employed a cockney joiner. Green, of course, was a self-taught amateur. His parents liked making things and had encouraged him in childhood. He'd made a boat and furniture in Durban. Beyond that he was woefully uneducated in woodwork.

He later admitted that he had surreptitiously learned a lot from the men he employed without, he thought, giving himself away. He also set about self-education, teaching himself, for example, how to cut rule joints and knuckle joint hinges. Hating the 'factory' mentality, and in flight from the imposed bell-dominated time schedules which beset schoolmasters, in his own workshop Green took pride in being a slow, thoughtful and painstaking worker.

He loved to saw and plane, regarding them as fine forms of exercise and great fun. He felt an affinity with wood and with nature believing that it is the responsibility of a craftsman to create beauty from natural resources. Witness his sonnet 'Tree Worship at the Bench':

By the sharp steel what wealth of ring and ray
  In convolutions new at every stroke
    Here first to human sight reveal'd of oak
Or walnut! - 'Cleave the wood,' His scriptures say,
  'And there am I' - This lustrous as the day,
    That as involved night! - days, nights, that broke
    Or fell on those fair groves where slept and woke
The gnarled giants, not vainly torn away.

To adorn man's dwelling, - May they teach to shoot
  His soul on such a shaft, so leafy bough'd
Into blue air, from every deep struck root
  Drawing slow nurture to a growth so proud,
And such interior loveliness minute
  Of ring and ray and ripple, light and cloud!

Since he had no grounding in design or architecture, Green began to use as a design method the only discipline in which he had been thoroughly trained: mathematics. He used angles, curves, lines, geometrical shapes, and the relationships between them, as the basis of both design and construction.

He began to find purity and loveliness in geometry as the Ancient Greeks did. '.............in a community for which geometry was a living subject not only to mathematicians but to artists and philosophers, as it was in Athens,' he wrote later in an article for *New English Weekly*, 'it would be at once realised that the designer who prefers a free-hand curve, or what is more likely a curve compounded of circular arcs when an easily drawn and truly geometric curve is available and at least equally beautiful has no music in his soul.'

Graham Castle, who was to work in Green's Christchurch workshop a quarter of a century later, believes that in this Green was decades ahead of his time. 'It is only now,' says Castle, a wise and elderly gentleman with a long and distinguished career in craft education behind him, 'that something similar to Green's geometrical designs are being produced on computers.'

But it was always difficult to make ends meet and Green spent most of his life subsisting from hand to mouth. To help out financially at Bosham various members of the family - Minnie Green, Florence's mother and sisters and even 'her formidable old father' - came to stay as paying guests, which helped. Green's old friend Gooch made him an allowance of £100 per year - a sort of private version of a modern enterprise grant.

Green's only child, Beatrice Romney Green, was born on 21st April 1901 - almost exactly four years after her parents were married. On his daughter's birth certificate Green's profession is given as 'schoolmaster', although he wasn't teaching at the time. Perhaps Florence preferred it to 'woodworker' for posterity. The baby's father, aged 29 years and three months, looks both back and forward in time in his charming 1901 poem 'To My Daughter Beatrice'.

> What glorious omens do attend thy birth
>   Fair child! - the fruit trees like a white sea foam
> Brake into flower with thee; the genial earth
>   Make haste with summer to adorn thy home.
>
> If by this golden earnest of his prime
>   Summer be judged - the harvest by the flower-
> Thus in the vaward of a beauteous time
>   Art surely come. - in this auspicious hour
>
> Just thirty years ago by thy grandsire
>   The tie was formed, the precious seed was sown,
> Of which heaven grant in thee to his desire
>   The fruit be seen, the virtue handed down;
>
> Ev'n as in that sweet crescent of the new
> The old moon glows. - O prove the omens true!

The birth, which took place at Critchfield, was a difficult one, stoically borne by Florence, now aged 36, with a fortitude which Green admired. He adored his daughter. For a man who, surprisingly for a teacher, doesn't seem to have liked children or enjoyed their company very much, this little girl was an exception. 'She was a great joy to me,' he wrote.

He remembered helping to nurse her after a serious illness. He was in the house, rather than at work, at the time because he too had been laid up with one of his usual bouts of bronchitis. He told Beatrice stories from his childhood, especially about his boat and the adventures he'd enjoyed in her. When, at last, Florence's doctor brother pronounced that the child was going to pull through the illness, Green burst into helpless tears of relief, rather to his wife's surprise.

Although the birth of Beatrice kept them fairly united for a further two or three years, the Greens' marriage was by now under strain. There were disagreements over the child and her future. Florence wanted to bring her up as a 'little lady'. Green had rather more egalitarian ambitions for her.

Green was becoming increasingly drawn by the socialist movement while Florence, the Tory, hated any mention of social reform. She, who had quite liked the poor-but-respectable status of being a schoolmaster's wife, regarded her husband's new role as socially inferior. So she was resentful. She rarely came into the workshop or showed any interest in his work there. And none of this, he felt, was helped by the renewal of frequent contact with her very worldly parents.

Green was rapidly falling out of love with Florence, although he never seems to have stopped feeling fond of her even when she exasperated him. 'My devotion was by this time so far from complete that I fell considerably in love with her beautiful youngest sister during one of her visits,' he records.

Critchfield House, Bosham, Hampshire.

Although Bosham was a fine place for sailing, Green could afford neither the time nor the money for boat building. He did, however, on one occasion, come close to winning a local regatta in a hired boat. Another time he sailed to Totland Bay with an acquaintance who had bought a cabin cruiser but who needed help with it. On the return journey the other man succumbed to seasickness and Green had to sail solo in a strong head wind and heavy seas on waters which, at that time, he hardly knew. They had prepared to spend the night in the lee of a headland near Cowes, on the Isle of Wight, before returning to Bosham the next morning.

Green loved writing - prose as well as poetry - and like most writers he was, by his own admission, fond of getting his work published and seeing his name in print. His first published writing was a letter he had written in his teens to a magazine, *Field*, commenting on the rating rules for yacht races. Then, while still at Cambridge, he had published an enthusiastic review of Lawrence Binyon's first volume of poems. He had also 'moonlighted' a little in Durban by freelancing for the *Natal Mercury*.

Now, settled to woodwork at Bosham, he wrote several long technical articles for *The Builder*. H. Statham was the editor and Green was introduced to him by his brother William. Green was gratified to be paid what seemed to him, by school teacher and woodworker standards, good fees for these contributions.

From the time that he set up in Bosham, and for most of the rest of his life, Green was to think of William as more like a father than a younger brother. The younger, more conventionally successful - and infinitely more conformist - Green would pass commissions to his elder brother and introduce him to useful people. And it is generally believed in the family that William - whom his children and grandchildren remembered as a generous man - regularly gave Romney cash when times were difficult.

The brothers were clearly attached to each other, their fondness based on a healthy mutual respect, but which didn't quite mean that either man really approved of the other's way of life. William had, by now, a growing family of his own. Five children were born between 1900 and 1910. His fourth child and third daughter, Joan, who was born in 1907 (and died in March 1997), was to become, in adult life, a warm admirer of her uncle as well as being a life-long friend of his daughter, her cousin Beatrice.

Green and Florence remained in Bosham for two years. Then it seemed to be time to move on.

Chapter 4: Haslemere and Socialism

Haslemere in Surrey had a lot to offer a craftsman in the early years of this century. Then something of a centre for craft, design and small industry, Haslemere already had hand-weaving and a cluster of other hand-work enterprises.

Also in the neighbourhood were Fred Green's old friends Sir Robert and Lady Hunter, who introduced Green and Florence to the local circle of cultured, and often wealthy, people - so Florence felt she was mixing in 'good company'. Green was anyway quite familiar with this green and pleasant region on the borders of Surrey and Hampshire because, as a boy, he had frequently stayed with the Hunters.

Green took a little workshop in Foundry Road, near Haslemere railway station. There he often met, and made friends with, the sort of company which Florence disliked - social reformers, social philosophers, pamphleteers and champions of 'bottom dogs'.

To begin with, the couple lived four miles north of the town in a rented house named 'Down End', at Hindhead. It was a highly scenic spot, not far from Devil's Punchbowl. Green and Beatrice enjoyed some longish walks near here, the father teaching his small daughter some of the poetry he'd enjoyed as a boy.

The Hindhead plan was that Florence should take boarders to generate income. She did so for a while but then found the work too much for her, so they moved to a smaller house at Haslemere, an aptly named cottage: 'Holdfast'. As usual, Green desperately wanted that Florence should manage the house without residential help. She tried and failed. So soon he had to give in.

The cottage was a mile and a half outside the town on the London road. A life-long cyclist, Green pedalled daily to his Haslemere workshop, first from Down End and then from Holdfast. He never owned a car nor wanted one. Comparing the bicycle with the car he wrote: 'The bicycle is a more elegant, more truly beautiful invention. Mr John Stewart Collis declares that it is the greatest invention of man. I rank it second only to the sailing boat, that still more wonderful creature. It is a miracle of balance, it gives you healthy exercise which a car denies, a wider range than that of the pedestrian, and leisure for every lovely view.'

Above: a chestnut bookcase. Below: a walnut bedstead.

He liked long distance cycling too and once cycled 130 miles home to Haslemere in a single day from Wednesbury in the West Midlands, not far from Great Barr where his in-laws, the Garmans, lived. He rode the first forty miles before breakfast. Then he ate home-cured ham at the Red Lion Inn at Long Compton before setting out to pedal the remaining 90 miles.

After several years at Holdfast, and not all that long before Green finally left Haslemere, the landlord served notice on them. Her husband suspected the cause might have been Florence's high-handed dealings with certain gamekeepers. Green had lost some money on the sale of his Durban house, although Bangley had done his best to get a good price. Nonetheless there was a little capital with which to buy a property - or build one. Green was enthusiastic because he was always excited at the prospect of creative experiment.

William or 'Will' to the family, but now publicly known as William Curtis Green, designed a beautiful cottage. Minnie helped by advancing Romney some money which she had been intending to bequeath to him. Green, of course did the woodwork. He made, for example, a splendid front door in oak for his new house which he once used as a 'visual aid' for a lecture on joinery at the Society of Arts in London. He took his door there in pieces on the train and reassembled it with a sledge hammer on stage!

Haslemere is a long way inland. For once Green had no ready access to water or sailing. This was a blow. Two or three sailing holidays in Cornwall and on the Norfolk Broads with his cousin, Ivor Tuckett, were some compensation.

Things went well in the workshop during the seven Haslemere years. Green found Arthur Terry working in a builder's workshop and hired him at first by the week and then as his first Haslemere employee. Terry was a country joiner. Like most of the apprentices and 'gentleman' pupils Green took on later, Terry was to develop into a furniture maker.

Worked in solid timbers with hand tools, items were made to designs produced either by Green or his brother. Many years later Graham Castle was to recall trying at Christchurch to construct to W. Curtis Green's designs: 'They looked fine but weren't always practicable to build. He didn't understand the finer points of woodwork. I remember one cabinet in particular. He hadn't made any provision for us to get the back on.'

Green's own designs, on the other hand, were practical as well as practicable if, at this early stage, not always artistically inspiring. One critic, for example, commented recently that a lot of Romney Green's tables are just copies of Elizabethan designs.

Ernest Gimson's visitor's book at his Sapperton workshop in the Cotswolds, shows that Green visited there in 1904 - presumably to learn. By then, Gimson - and Sidney Barnsley nearby - had made names for themselves as innovative designer craftsmen working in solid timbers with hand tools. Green adheres to many of the 'Cotswold' principles. He may have been introduced to Gimson by his brother William, who occasionally collaborated with Gimson on projects - such as the designing, building and furnishing of a house near Cambridge in 1907.

Green's work was soon being shown by the Arts and Crafts Exhibition Society. The 1903 and 1906 catalogues, for example, list a corner cupboard in Spanish chestnut, designed by W. Curtis Green priced at 6 guineas (£6.30). There was also an oak sideboard at £22.15s (£22.75) and an oak table at 6 guineas. These last two were designed by Green. The tables he had made himself while the sideboard was 'executed' by D.D. Dillaway, one of his employees.

The Board of Trade showed his work at international exhibitions. A bookcase in oak, with a mathematically arched top, four shelves and a cupboard at the base, was exhibited at Milan where it won a silver medal. Green also made a number of pieces, including a refectory table and a wardrobe, designed by his brother for their second cousin, Debell Tuckett's new house at Netherton in Devon. Tuckett became, and remained, a loyal customer and friend. Work continued at Netherton until 1926.

There was evidently a certain amount of local trade too. Mr A.E. Howarth, who lives in South London, has written to the author to say that he has two Romney Green oak bedsteads, one heavily chip-carved. A third, much plainer, one was donated by Mr Howarth to the Lutyens Trust. These bedsteads were purchased by Mr Howarth's grandparents when they lived in Haslemere at the beginning of the twentieth century.

Having begun at Haslemere with just one or two employees, Green eventually built up to a complement of six, plus pupils Bernard Unwin and Michael Halward. Henry Pleming, although 'working class', became a dear friend. Pleming was an excellent joiner and immensely strong. He also shared Green's love of poetry, socialism and bicycles and the two men undertook a tour round England together. It included Green's showing Pleming round Sidney Sussex College as they passed through Cambridge and, at one point, the two cyclists being obliged to spend the night in a double bed. When Green finally left Haslemere and went to London, the loyal Pleming moved with him.

Green freely acknowledged that, although the workshop did fairly well, it was never quite financially secure. This, he believed, was owing to his refusal ever to devote himself wholly to one thing. Although he worked hard at his woodwork business he also continued to write and publish articles.

For example, William suggested that Green should enter an essay competition for a prize offered by the Royal Institute of British Architects (RIBA). The subject was The Development of Architectural Art from Structural Requirements and the Nature of the Material. Green wrote a piece attacking the growing acceptance of iron ties or girders and ferro-concrete in buildings of architectural pretension. In 1905 he was delighted to be offered a special prize for his work. 'I wish I had known you earlier,' quipped his brother, the up-and-coming architect. *The British Architect* published Green's prize winning essay in two parts on 16th and 23rd July 1909.

Green's first book was called simply *Poems* and was published in November 1901 in a limited edition by The Astolat Press in Guildford. The press was owned by a relative, A.C. Curtis. Seven 'special' copies of the edition were published on Japanese vellum and a further 500 on handmade paper. The traditional slim volume included 'Natal: An Ode', 'To My Daughter Beatrice', 'To My Wife', other love poems to, or about, Florence and a translation from Ovid which he'd made in Durban.

It was at Haslemere that Green first met Percival Strong who became his doctor and life-long friend. Strong was playing Theseus in a performance of *A Midsummer Night's Dream* in the rectory garden. Green was very taken with his splendid stature and the way in which he rolled out Shakespeare's verse. Later Green recognised just how sensitive was this kindly and thoughtful man to the needs and suffering of his poorer patients, who 'naturally adored him'.

A reserved but Romantic man, Strong revelled in literature, art, music and natural scenery. Florence came to love him, but his relationship with her didn't mature. He never married although he had several women friends. After he had left Haslemere to practise elsewhere - his asthma was a limitation - he and Green corresponded and met regularly until Strong's death in the early 1940s.

Green always argued that it would have been perfectly possible, in Edwardian England, to make a reasonable living from a designer-woodwork business for anyone willing to 'specialise' by dropping all other activities. For himself he preferred to diversify.

Once a teacher always a teacher. Green frequently drifted back into peripatetic or part-time teaching at different stages of his life if there was an interesting post available or if he needed to augment his income. He occasionally took on private tuition too. While living at Haslemere, in about 1906, he was 'headhunted' by the two local headmistresses who had heard him speak at a political meeting. They persuaded him to turn from the workshop to teach a few hours per week of mathematics and woodwork in their girls' school, St George's Wood, which he seems to have enjoyed. When eventually his 'disgrace' became public knowledge, and he was about to leave Haslemere, of course the mistresses at the school reluctantly decided that they could no longer employ him. So impressed by him were they, however, that they offered - perhaps as a sort of apology in kind - to educate his daughter Beatrice free. She remained at St George's Wood until she reached university age. Green's brother William then financed her through university.

The other major interest at Haslemere with which the workshop had to share his attention was Green's growing interest in socialism.

Harold Murray, a dentist, and his wife Bertha were socialists who had arrived at Haslemere with their two children not long after the Greens' move there. Green, wanting to be active in their cause, was instantly drawn to them. Florence, on the other hand, unsurprisingly took an instant dislike to the Murrays whom, knowing their political views, she perjoratively regarded as 'Bohemian'.

Green and Murray started an Independent Labour Party (ILP) group which met in the showroom above Green's workshop. Sometimes as many as 40 or 50 people attended the meetings: a mixture of small tradesmen, artisans, the men who worked for Green and, sometimes, a sprinkling of local bigwigs. Speakers came down from London, including Henry Golding who became a close and dear friend to Green. They even organised a debate in Haslemere Town Hall between Ramsay MacDonald and John St Loe Strachey, editor of *The Spectator*. This, they believed, was the first important debate on socialism to be held outside London.

William Beveridge lived locally. Later Lord Beveridge, and with a life of distinguished public service ahead of him, he was still only in his twenties when Green knew him. From 1903 Beveridge was leader writer on social problems for *The Morning Post* and already something of a celebrity. His unmathematical theories about trade fluctuations vexed Green, the mathematician, who played tennis with Beveridge's mother and sister, but who always regarded himself as a distinctly peripheral acquaintance to Beveridge.

Another neighbour, Richard Henry (R.H.) Tawney, had been at Balliol College, Oxford with Beveridge. Tawney was to become an influential 'left-wing' historian who influenced the thoughts and philosophy of the developing Labour movement. He joined ILP in 1909.

As a delegate of 'his' ILP branch, Green attended League meetings in London. There he met Josiah Clement Wedgwood, descendant of the founder of the Wedgwood pottery. Wedgwood, later Lord Wedgwood, was to be first a Liberal, and then a famous Labour, politician between the wars. Green read Wedgwood's slim book *The Road to Freedom.* At the same time he and Murray were also reading the writings of Arthur Kitson and becoming interested in theories of money reform. Green was also much impressed by *Where Men Decay* by Lieut. Col. D.C. Pedder.

Green dissented from some 'orthodox' socialist views however and argued with Bertrand Russell, his exact contemporary in age, in a lengthy correspondence. Russell, with *An Essay on the Foundations of Geometry* (1897) and *The Principles of Mathematics* (1903) already behind him, believed that you can apply mathematical reasoning to the solutions of ethical and political problems. But, unlike William Morris and John Ruskin, Green argued that it should always be the creative impulse which provides men and women with the incentive to labour. All his life he criticised humanity's obsessive drive to invent and build machines which would deprive men of the dignity and pleasure of creative employment. 'When the creative impulse is denied its most natural outlet in healthy productive labour it tends to atrophy and the appetites which cannot be thus disused and atrophied step in to fill the gap,' he wrote.

He detested the pessimistic and utilitarian views expressed in *Modern Utopia* by H.G. Wells, whom he met for discussions in London. For Green every activity had to be worth doing for its own sake. He had no truck with arguments in favour of regarding everything that you do merely as a means to some other end.

The usual socialist notion that the troubles of the world are all rooted in the employers' desire for profits, he found too simplistic. Getting rid of competition, nationalising industry and re-employing employers as salaried servants of the State - as advocated by a faction he condemnatorily described as Fabians, Philistines and Utilitarians - would solve nothing, Green believed.

Bertha Murray.

Rather he favoured imaginative solutions - such as running workhouses as self-supporting co-operatives and looking for ways in which society's 'bottom dogs' could make a living.

Of course Green was himself an employer, although ironically self-depreciating about it. When he and Pleming undertook their cycle tour of English cathedral cities, Pleming turned back at Ely because he was the 'wage slave' and had to get back to the workshop. Green, with 'the comparative freedom, however poverty stricken, of the small working master who can trust his staff,' pedalled joyfully on into Yorkshire and returned to Surrey via Gloucester, Tewkesbury and Worcester.

Then came 'the crash' - his own term for the momentous decision which altered everything and changed the rest of Green's life instantly and irrevocably. It cost him his home, a share in the rest of his daughter's childhood, much of his livelihood, his fragile 'respectability', most of his friends and acquaintances and, at least temporarily, the respect of his beloved mother and siblings.

When Romney Green left Haslemere and deserted Florence to set up home with Bertha Murray he was, indeed, staking all he had, as he said later. But he never regretted it for a second.

Chapter 5: The Crash

Bertha Anne Murray, nee Morris, was the great love of Green's life. She was, by all accounts, a beautiful woman. Her personality was warm and compelling and it attracted most people who met her. She was highly intelligent and a fine musician. Tall and slender with high cheek bones and slightly wan, she looks startlingly like Virginia Woolf in surviving photographs and drawings. Her 'story' of a sexually alert, unhappily married woman in love who abandons home, husband and family, is reminiscent of that of another contemporary - D.H. Lawrence's wife, Frieda.

Much later, during the First World War, Green and Bertha spent two or three days in close proximity to the Lawrences in Essex. Green, who had already read several of Lawrence's novels and knew his poetry, found the 'sex-obsessed' writer to be a shallow thinker - neither pagan nor happy and, in fact, rather boring. Frieda Lawrence was famously and serially unfaithful to the man she left her husband for. Interestingly, those who knew Bertha evidently expected her 'free' life to follow a similar pattern. But they were wrong. After Bertha's death in 1942 one of her relations expressed surprise to Green that Bertha had remained totally faithful to him for the whole of their thirty-two years together.

Green was 30 when he first met Bertha at Haslemere in 1902. She was four years older than Green and had already been married to Harold Murray since 1885, having been more or less coerced into marriage as a fresh-faced 17-year old with large, pretty blue eyes. Murray, who was eight years older than Bertha, had regarded them as engaged since Bertha's thirteenth birthday. Green believed that she had finally succumbed to marriage four years later only because Murray had been seriously ill and applied emotional pressure to a girl too young to be assertive enough to resist.

For some years after their marriage the Murrays lived at Hampstead in the late 1880s and early 1890s. Murray, a dentist, built up a successful practice there. Nearby lived Harold's brother Oswald, whose wife Louise also found difficulty with 'the masterful Murray temperament.' Bertha and Louise became close friends and remained in touch even after Bertha had left Harold.

Bertha could never return the passionate and possessive love of her husband either physically or emotionally. She could only pretend - and her pretence was often unconvincing. 'The ruin of half the marriages comes from the man demanding every bit the woman has to give . . . Oh I got so sick of it,' she wrote later.

Roger Fry painted the Murray's son, Eric, when he was a little boy. Bertha became so friendly with Fry that their relationship was verging on a love affair - and this was just one of several incidents which gave Harold Murray cause for jealousy. That is probably why he suddenly decided to move his family to California, abandoning dentistry, of which he professed himself tired, in order to take up fruit farming.

It was a hard life. Murray worked long days on the farm and eventually built a good adobe house for his family. Bertha had her Bechstein piano there but little time to play it. Not only did she do all the washing, scrubbing and cleaning for a household of four or five, including her young son Eric, but she also worked for long hours outside on the fruit farm.

She loved the romance of the beautiful flower-covered hills in which they sometimes camped out. During one of these excursions she began a love affair with their 'aide-de-camp' whose name was Alan. Green knew and recorded very little about Alan, wishing after her death that he'd asked Bertha more about him and her other 'lovers'. He takes it for granted that they must have existed.

At first the Murrays' farming venture was reasonably successful, but in the last years of the nineteenth century they had a run of typically Californian bad luck, including droughts and burst water dams. Harold became seriously ill with overwork and was taken by a friend for what was supposed to be a fortnight's holiday on the Western coast. Bertha was left in sole charge. She and Eric, by then aged about 11, had to feed the horses and ride them, as well as dealing single-handedly with hazards such as rattlesnakes. In the event Harold was away for six long and difficult weeks.

Murray, by then in serious financial difficulties, was obliged to accept the managership of a small gold mine, living meanwhile in a nearby shanty with his wife and son. He ran the mine without any other staff and he and Bertha installed the electric machinery themselves. Each evening she manned the machines for a five hour shift while her husband got some sleep. There, in the shanty, their second child, Esther, was born. Murray delivered his daughter himself because there was no medical support available.

Then the proprietor of the mine defrauded Murray out of a year's salary. This completed their ruin. The couple - with a son in his early teens and a

37

new baby daughter - returned to England, probably in 1902 , with the help of their old friend Godfrey Blount. They had to leave behind the piano, their library of books and almost everything else they had of value. It was at Blount's house in Haslemere that Green first met them.

Green was instantly struck by Bertha's revealing and beautiful eyes, although unsurprisingly after her Californian experiences, she looked, in her late thirties, like a woman marred by suffering and hard work. The youthful bloom had gone, although in time her relationship with Green engendered another sort of beauty, rooted in mature serenity. As Louise Murray wrote many years later to Green: 'Your great love, that contemplative artistic nature of yours, became for her an initiation.'

In Haslemere Murray once more began to practise dentistry, quickly building up a reasonable business at 2 Station Chambers. The family lived in a small cottage where Green soon became a regular visitor as he and Murray, twelve years his senior, discussed their socialist plans and ideas. The impoverished Murrays had no domestic help, a way of living which Green, predictably, admired very much.

For the first two years of his knowing the Murrays, Green believed that they were happily married. He and Harold talked socialism in the kitchen while Bertha prepared supper. The meals were quite simple although nothing ever seemed too much trouble to her.

Then the Murrays moved to a larger house and took on a maid. They held meetings there for up to twenty people, to whom Bertha calmly served refreshments. Green was struck by her competence. Although she didn't join in the conversation much he noticed that her face was often lit up by spontaneous remarks. As she and her husband grew more prosperous she dressed better. Green admired her fine taste and fondly recalled her reclining on a sofa in the evenings, wearing a blue dressing gown and smoking the occasional cigarette - but never in front of her daughter or the maid. She had an elegant gait and a perfectly proportioned figure. As a dutiful Edwardian wife she would, for her husband's sake, occasionally don a veil and kid gloves and make a social call.

All this Green observed as a family friend. Then the truth was eventually revealed when Murray happened, in an unguarded moment, to confide that all was not well in his marriage. 'That unloosed the floodgates of my love and pity for this adorable woman,' wrote Green.

One summer day - probably in 1904 - Green spent a day in London with the Murrays whilst Florence was holidaying, with Beatrice, at her parents' home in the Midlands - as she did most years. This was the memorable day that the three of them decided on the mutual use of Christian names. Extraordinary as it seems today, they had hitherto been addressing each other as 'Mr Green' and 'Mr and Mrs Murray'.

Green and Bertha went to a Blake exhibition in the morning while Harold did some business: it was the first time that they had been alone together. Green was charmed by her wit and gaiety. After lunch with Murray, they all three went to a matinee performance of Shaw's *You Never Can Tell* and ended the day with a tour of the Austrian Exhibition at Earl's Court.

A few days later he had a 'gratifying but perplexing' little talk with Bertha at a socialist garden party, after which he left for a weekend's holiday with his mother and a Quaker aunt at Ventnor. Green later regarded the summer Sunday he spent in 1904 on the waters of the Isle of Wight as 'the last day of entirely innocent unthinking happiness in my life, though it was so soon succeeded by days of triumphal happiness such as I had never known nor dreamed of.'

And so they acknowledged their love for each other - not physically at first but gently, intellectually and romantically. On the Monday morning he found a note from Bertha awaiting him at the workshop. It was ostensibly about work - a wooden chest - but it had a subtext. So did Green's reply which Murray read and then angrily confronted the pair with - although he was fairly easily persuaded that he had overacted. Thereafter Murray had to be deceived, although both lovers, each of them extraordinarily truthful by nature, hated the necessity for this.

Green quotes a very intimate and a poignant letter from Bertha - who loved the old intimate pronoun forms and often addressed Green by a pet name, 'Boy'. The letter gives a clear picture of her agonised dilemma.

'I too this morning went through an awful time before getting up. Harold begged me to stay after Babbie [Esther] had gone, and then took me in his arms most tenderly and begged me, prayed me, to try to love him better. He went through all the past, the years of absolute devotion, and asked me so pitifully what he could do to stir my soul as it could be stirred (as thou has stirred it, my loved Romney). He asked me, knowing him as I do, would I still marry him? I said, knowing what I do now, I would never marry any man without ties or duty; that I hated duty, it had nothing to do with love. Then he said , 'Would I be the man? Then came the ghastly lie, "I know no other." O Boy, Boy, what I would have given to speak the truth - to say, in Romney Green I have found my heart's desire - but it would have killed him.'

Drawing of Bertha, artist unknown.

Drawing of Arthur Romney Green, artist unknown.

Green describes their first real sexual encounter - or Great Occasion - with moving candour. They waited a long time because they both had 'proper respect for the rites of love.' The place and the time had to be right. Nothing furtive would do. Everything was to be 'frank and lovely with Aphrodite new-risen from the sea.'

They met in a lighted room - not in a bedroom - where she dropped her blue dressing gown and curtsied 'with half shy but alluring grace.' Then when they were ready she lay back on the sofa with her long white arms behind her head.' But alas, consummation wasn't to be, because on this occasion he was impotent, a situation which very few men would write about for posterity to read. Happily 'never again had my lovely Bertha to suffer that unprecedented mortification.'

The quite erotic sonnet 'Green Places', inspired by his love for Bertha, is one of Green's most effective poems:

> Ah, how I love the silver shining boughs
>   And golden glooms of those green places where,
>   With sunlight, moonlight, starlight in your hair,
> And in your eyes beneath those arched brows
> A fire of such deep love as might arose
>   The dead, you came, and were so heavenly fair,
>   And with such passion listen'd to my prayer,
> Nor hope witheld, and listen'd to my vows
>
>
> But half-believing. - you, of all comrades first
> And women fairest, you whose eyes conversed
>   With mine above the throng, and spake so plain,
>   And pledged the draught I live, or die to drain -
> Come thus, if only thus, to quench my thirst-
>   O come to those green places once again.

They were to make love as often as they could during the five years or so of their clandestine affair - in the workshop, in the room behind the showroom, outdoors and, to Green's chagrin, occasionally at Bertha's home in her husband's absence. Sometimes the intervals were necessarily long and several times they tried deliberately to abstain from encounters with each other in an attempt to break things off for the sake of their families. At one stage Green 'fled' on some pretext with Florence and Beatrice to a cottage at Fernhurst to put himself out of temptation's way, but Florence didn't like the isolation so they returned.

As well as three or four letters a week, he wrote much poetry to and about Bertha as he would for the rest of his life. The following is an extract from one of the first:

You gave me of your heavenly store
Love, beauty - ay, and wisdom more
Than mortal where attended least;
The earthly fire, the heavenly ore
Love the arch-tempter, love the priest
Passionate joy, the pagan's lore
With all the wisdom of the East
Enrich'd and chastened - this I found
Where only sin is thought to be,
The Christ made manifest in thee
In thee the Roman Venus crown'd,
Fire, but the unconsumed Tree
Still green upon that holy ground.

Bertha professed to prefer receiving letters to poems. Knowing that, as recently as late as 1901, he had published some of the love poems he had written to Florence, she suspected that his poetry was too glib to be a sincere expression of personal feeling. But sometimes he did 'reach' Bertha with poetry, especially when it was understated. Of his sonnet 'A Tryst' she wrote 'Boy, Boy, this poem is divine. It shall be <u>ours</u>, dear; there is the human touch only to make the whole complete and perfect - no personal ecstasies - ah, bless thee.'

A Tryst

Out of the fog we climb'd to what a tryst
    Through heath and brake and briar! The drenching dews
    Sun touch'd on every spray with iris hues
Alight the drifting many-colour'd mist,
Woods, hills like wine in the antique amethyst
    Our draught of golden browns and violet blues!-
    Drink deep, as't were the last, we lot to lose
A drop from this clear chalice:- we, sun-kissed,

And blest out of the blue in this high place:
    The world its coils and dragon scales below,
    Deep-lost, through plotting years of weal or woe
To crown or to condemn an hour of grace:
    Which, who would ask, - who fear to undergo
Whatever fate attends your heaven-lit face?

Florence had always insisted that her marriage to Green was to be 'open' and 'free' which left her scope for the flirtations she so enjoyed, as and when she wanted them. At about the same time that Green was becoming seriously involved with Bertha, Florence was, for example spending time with Green's life-long doctor friend, Percival Strong. But for her none of it was serious and she regarded her marriage as a permanence. Thus when she first became aware that Green was falling in love with Bertha she was almost glad and expressed sympathy, although she had never like the 'Bohemian' Murrays. Not until she realised that the situation was threatening her marriage, did she become alarmed or in any way jealous.

It's also worth mentioning, moreover, that Green hadn't stopped loving her. He was deeply in love with Bertha but that didn't mean that he couldn't also love Florence in a different way. 'Passionately as I loved Bertha, I had not ceased to love my wife: every poet has known, even though every woman may have denied it, that it is possible for a man to love two women at the same time. I was naturally distressed by the thought of leaving my wife.'

Then the blow fell. Harold Murray found out what was going on. After various abortive attempts at mediation and compromise, in the spring of 1909 Green and Bertha left Haslemere at the same time, but separately.

Florence and Murray were both profoundly damaged and became bitter, working out their hurt in different ways. Florence refused to divorce Green for nearly twenty years so he was not free to marry Bertha until 1928, by which time he was 55 and she was 59. And Green didn't see his daughter Beatrice again until she was grown up.

Bertha's 'punishment' was crueller. Murray did divorce her quite quickly and he remarried, although the fierce possessive love he'd had for Bertha for so long burned on for the rest of his life. But Bertha never saw Esther again. Leaving her as a child of 7 or 8 she was, like Frieda Lawrence, denied all access to her daughter. The only news she heard came occasionally from her friend, Mabel Cox. Later on, when Esther was grown up, Bertha's former sister-in-law, Louise Murray, almost persuaded Esther to break the promise that she had made her father that she would never make contact with her mother - but not quite.

After Bertha's death Green was moved almost beyond words to find, wrapped in tissue paper, a tiny pair of Esther's woollen gloves. Bertha had brought them away from Haslemere with her and kept them secretly as a poignant memento for thirty-one years in the treasure box which Green had so lovingly made her. At the time of Bertha's death in 1942 her 'baby' daughter, by then a successful international secretary, would have been a woman of over 40.

Bertha's 'Treasure Box'.

Bertha was luckier with her son Eric, who was already living and working independently in Central America when his mother left home. She corresponded with Eric for the rest of her life, although for geographical reasons they never met again. He remained and prospered abroad. She 'knew' his wife and her grandchildren from letters.

Of course 'the crash' had professional repercussions too. Green had just been proposed as a Member of the Senior Art Worker's Guild where he would have been able to mix with 'names' such as Ernest Gimson, Sidney Barnsley and Paul Cooper. Membership would have increased his credibility and would undoubtedly have helped him to become better known as a furniture designer and maker. The proposal was withdrawn as soon as his leaving his wife for another woman was known.

Just before 'the crash' Green had also been invited, at his mother's instigation and to her delight, to deliver the annual address to the deacons of the Diocese of Southwark. As things turned out he was not, inevitably, allowed to appear in person to deliver 'Socialism as a Religious Cause', but he was pleased that the Archdeacon of Southwark read it out on his behalf.

Then there was a well attended lecture to the Fabian Education Group at Cliffords Inn in 1908. Rev. Stuart Headlam chaired the meeting and R.H. Tawney hovered - with patronising nonchalance - in the doorway while Green attacked the sort of Socialism espoused by Ramsay MacDonald and anyone else who regarded himself as what Green ironically termed 'a moral person'. Green argued passionately that the quality of creative or artistic life is more important than life itself and that there is no point in preserving life indiscriminately if the only life you can offer is based on miserable utilitarianism. This stance was not popular, and although Ramsay MacDonald promised to print Green's lecture in *Socialist Monthly*, Green thought that MacDonald was relieved to have an excuse to drop it when Green's 'disgrace' became known.

Green's plan was to 'begin again' in London and to find a way in which he and Bertha could be there together. His Haslemere workshop was taken over by his foreman Arthur Terry, assisted by Michael Halward. They ran it successfully until the outbreak of war in 1914. Green, meanwhile, set off in search of his new life, but there were plenty of difficulties to overcome first.

Chapter 6: London and the First World War

On first leaving Haslemere Bertha stayed part of the time with some friends - Oswald and Mabel Cox - who lived at Hawthorn Cottage in Hampstead. She also stayed for a while at Alfriston in Sussex in a country cottage belonging to another friend Mr Aitkins, Director of the Tate Gallery. To keep herself busy she polished the 'dirty' oak furniture which it was Mr Aitkins's hobby to collect. Harold Murray sent her money, in return for a promise that she would not see Green.

For several weeks the lovers communicated only by letter. They missed each other desperately but needed what would now be called 'space' to work out exactly what they were going to do next, each trying to dissuade the other from a rash decision. 'Thy haggard face haunts me,' wrote Bertha from Alfriston. 'I can see thee alone at the workshop and homeless too and, Boy, I long to mother thee, long till my very stomach aches. But, Boy, it is the price we have to pay; we have often spoken of it; bravely, fearlessly. Let us not fail in it; our future happiness depends on it.'

While still in Haslemere, Green had built up what would now be called 'good contacts' amongst the London Arts and Crafts 'set'. And it was they, especially Herbert Spencer and Gertrude Spink, who found for Green a little two-bench workshop in a converted stable at Hammersmith Terrace, only about five miles away from the house he'd been born in 37 years earlier. There is nothing now answering this description in Hammersmith Terrace itself which comprises a splendid, unspoiled line of 16 Georgian houses backing onto the Thames. Green may mean a tiny corner property abutting a cottage where the Terrace joins Black Lion Lane, opposite the centuries-old Black Lion pub. It would probably have had rear access onto Hammersmith Terrace in Green's time.

Green's bench stood in one corner of the workshop, which had formerly been occupied by the young Eric Gill, who had lived for two years with his wife in a cottage, now demolished, at 20 Black Lion Lane. An elderly employee called Lewis, once employed by William Morris, worked at the other. The premises - in which Green wasn't supposed to sleep because there was no lavatory - had a loft above and a small yard and garden at the back. Spencer and Spink helped to find trade for Green.

And he certainly needed such help because money was very short. The allowance from Gooch stopped at the time of 'the crash'. Green had left almost everything he owned with Florence and was, in a sense, pleased to do so because it helped to assuage the guilt.

Hammersmith at that time was an ideal place for a man of Green's temperament and outlook. It was an artistically vibrant environment because a surprising number of 'intellectual craftsmen' worked there just before the First World War. Kelmscott House, home of William Morris, was just two or three minutes' walk along the riverside and Morris's legacy was still strong in Hammersmith in 1909. T.J. Cobden-Sanderson, founder of Doves Press and close collaborator with him, was a near neighbour of Morris and still there while Green was a resident. Although Gill had moved out before Green's arrival, it was probably at Hammersmith that the two men met for the first time.

Douglas (later Hilary after his conversion from Quakerism to Catholicism in 1917) Pepler, catalyst to many Arts and Crafts adherents, lived with his family at 14 Hammersmith Terrace. Edward Johnston, calligrapher and designer of letters, lived at No. 3. May Morris, William's daughter, was at No. 8 and Emery Walker, a printer who had worked with Morris, at No. 7. Much of Hammersmith Terrace was occupied by Arts and Crafts practitioners. Arthur Penty, author of *The Restoration of the Gild System* lived nearby. Hammersmith artists such as Frank Brangwyn, Muirhead Bone and William Richmond showed work in the Annual Picture Exhibition with crafts from T.J. Cobden-Sanderson, May Morris, Johnston and Gill.

Harold Monro, publisher and poet, and his wife Dorothy, whom Green had known in Haslemere, now became good friends to Bertha and Green. Later, after Dorothy had left Monro to live with someone else and Harold had married Alida Klementaski, Green and Bertha remained close friends with all four. Monro's Poetry Bookshop, founded in 1913, published and sold works by contemporary poets and also arranged public readings of their work. Green gave a reading at one of these meetings and Monro published several of his poems as well as encouraging him to write literary essays and articles.

But Green's family and many of his Haslemere friends were horrified by his leaving Florence. The reaction and pain of upright and conventional William, three years younger than Romney, who had always revered his beloved elder brother has reverberated down the generations of his family to the present day. William, very serious, had travelled with Frederick Curtis, Margaret's husband, Romney's cousin and brother-in-law, to Haslemere as soon as 'the crash' threatened. They had done their best to talk Green out of his intention to leave his wife. Debell

Tuckett, second cousin and client, had offered Green a year's holiday in Switzerland to get him away from 'temptation'.

Green visited his mother Minnie and sister Margaret at Redhill, contrite and desperately unhappy about causing pain to those he loved, but by then he was quite unable to do what they really wanted of him. A letter from Bertha counselled: 'I agree that your poor mother's pain is the cruellest of all. Write to her every day simply and tenderly, not elaborate letters but love letters, with every promise you can truly make to still live a better life than you have yet been able to do.'

Then Gertrude Spink offered Bertha a job at The Artificers' Guild Gallery in Maddox Street, off Regent Street in London's West End. She accepted, told Spink the truth about her situation because she wanted no misunderstandings, and got Mabel Cox to help her make a brown overall for the work. The plan was that she should find a single furnished room or lodge at the Coxes, although Green was encouraged to visit her at the gallery during her lunch hour.

After only a week or two of this work Bertha fell ill. This gave Green the excuse he needed to move her as soon as she was well enough to his 'own lair'. Thereafter they were to live together as man and wife until Bertha's death in 1942.

Because the workshop was officially 'insanitary' they lodged with a Mr and Mrs Darnell nearby for a few weeks. Then, when Bertha was better, they slipped illegally back to live at the workshop where Bertha set up a stove in the loft and they 'practised rural hygiene' in the garden. At one point they had so little money that they were reduced to a regular diet of dates and dry biscuits for breakfast.

Of course they now slept together. Lewis made them the deal bed, painted green, which Green and Bertha were to share for the next 32 years. With his usual reverential approach to sex Green records that he made love to Bertha as often as she would allow it. It was she who 'wisely' limited the frequency of their Great Occasions, presumably because of their common belief that sexual joy should be prized and never taken for granted. Green agreed with Bertrand Russell's argument in his *Conquest of Happiness* that, far from being something innately wicked, sex is 'the greatest joy that life has to offer.'

Green would have liked another child, especially a son of Bertha's, but he also recognised that in their near-homeless impoverishment a family would have been a 'very millstone'. One of them - probably Bertha, who at 42 was almost certainly still of child-bearing age - must also therefore have kept a close eye on the calendar because no child was conceived.

Determined to do her bit to earn some money, Bertha took to looking after the neighbouring Peplers' children for two or three hours each afternoon and Green remembered how they enjoyed dangling toys on strings through the holes in the loft floor so that he could see them from his bench below. Sometimes the Johnston children came too. Perhaps this work helped Bertha cope with the ache she must have felt for her own 'lost' child, Esther. Green recorded how Bertha made two or three sad attempts to set up 'chance' meetings with Esther during the years they lived in London. She never succeeded.

Their first year or two together was not always easy. Both still felt a painful mixture of guilt, loving affection and sympathy towards the partners they had left. Green even sent Florence occasional letters. 'I was miserable on her account,' he wrote. There was silence from Florence. Even at this early stage Green was hoping that Florence's relationship with Percival Strong might develop so that there could be a divorce which would free him to remarry. But it wasn't to be.

Before too long Green's family began to come to terms with the situation and, when she was in London, Minnie Green soon began to visit them regularly, thus getting to know Bertha and becoming fond of her. William, and Margaret, saw Green too but felt unable to invite him and Bertha to their homes lest the children be corrupted. Green therefore saw very little of his nieces and nephews until they were old enough to decide for themselves whether to associate with their 'reprobate' uncle. Something of this 'compromise' seems to have carried down into the next generation too. Joan Yeo, William's daughter, loved and admired her Uncle Romney, corresponded with him, visited him and acted as his literary executor after his death. Yet none of Joan Yeo's three children have any memory of meeting their great uncle when he was an old man and they were children during the Second World War - presumably because their mother discreetly ensured that they didn't.

Because he often felt unhappy in the early months in London, Green plunged himself into bench work, soon assisted by the loyal Pleming who came up to Hammersmith to join him. Pleming disliked the London dirt and noise and certainly didn't want that for his wife and daughter, so it wasn't long before he moved his family back to the country. Nonetheless Green was touched and encouraged by the solidarity implicit in Pleming's choosing to work for/with him again for a while.

Having already exhibited at the Arts and Crafts Exhibition Society's exhibitions of 1903 and 1906 while he was at Haslemere, Green - now London based - showed two more pieces in 1910, five in 1912 and three in 1916. He would continue to exhibit at each exhibition until 1935 and was, as research by Dr Matthew Denney of Southampton Institute shows, actually the third most prolific exhibitor between 1877 and 1935 after Ernest Gimson and Ambrose Heal. About half of Green's exhibition pieces were chairs and dining tables.

Green also worked long hours at what he rather pompously called his 'literary work' in the evenings. He worried afterwards that this had led him to neglect Bertha at a time when she must surely have been feeling quite vulnerable. He continued to churn out articles and poems - although not much was published at this time because Green was no longer regarded as 'respectable' by editors. Bertha, for her part, never took his writing as seriously as she did his bench work. For Green they had equal parity.

When he wasn't working they enjoyed reading together. She liked Emerson, Neitzsche and Shaw. Green shared her enthusiasm for the first two, but was less comfortable with Shaw. Green had left the ILP behind in Haslemere and was now seriously doubtful about the sort of 'orthodox' Socialist solutions espoused by Shaw.

They also enjoyed jaunts to Richmond Park and Kew Gardens and went several times to Stock in Essex where Bertha's elderly father, confusingly called William Morris, lived with his second wife, Bessie, amongst pigs and hens. Green and Bertha also attended Sunday morning gatherings at Hampshire House in Hammersmith, getting to know ever more people, most of whom knew the truth of their 'situation' but cheerfully accepted them as they were.

Then one evening, after they had been in London for about a year, Bertha suffered the first 'attack' of the cardiac asthma from which she was to suffer for the rest of her life. It was winter and bitterly cold. Already tired, Bertha had, unusually, gone out alone. A stranger brought her back to Hammersmith Terrace, gasping for breath and unable to stand. With help from Dorothy Monro, Clare Pepler and Greta Johnston, Green nursed her for about three weeks in the loft over the workshop which now served them as a bedroom. No sooner was Bertha recovered than Green was himself laid up for several weeks with one of his frequent bouts of bronchitis.

Harold Monro then generously invited Green and Bertha to stay in his house on Lake Maggiore at Ascona in Italy for six weeks' convalescent holiday. In a Romantic idyll, which sounds reminiscent of William

Wordsworth and his sister Dorothy excitedly bouncing ideas back and forth with Coleridge in rural Somerset over a century earlier, Green, Bertha and Monro walked through the hills to picturesque villages. In the evenings they wrote 'vigorous' poems and read them aloud to each other. Back in London friends were regrouping. The Peplers and the Johnstons moved into another sort of craftsmen's colony at Ditchling in Sussex, where Gill by now had his little farm as well as his workshop. Ethel Mairet was producing her well-known fabrics there, much admired by Bertha, and Pepler set up his printing press. Green and Bertha several times cycled the forty miles from London to Ditchling, in spite of Bertha's heart trouble.

And this was where they first met Philip Mairet. Another 'Renaissance man' like Green, Mairet had an established reputation as an artist in stained glass, but at Ditchling he was also writing, gardening, bee keeping and using his architectural training in the building of a concrete house. A fine singer, Mairet later worked for a while as a professional actor at The Old Vic. He opened a handicraft gallery in Percy Street and eventually became editor of *New English Weekly* after the death of its founding editor, Alfred Richard Orage, in 1932. Mairet published a great deal of Green's writing in *New English Weekly* during the last decade or so of Green's life.

Now that the Hammersmith Terrace community was beginning to break up, Gertrude Spink took over an eighteenth century former pub a few miles further up-river, The Old Ship Inn, at 56 Strand-on-the-Green. Green and Bertha shared it with her. Spink had a workshop on the ground floor and so did Green. Bertha and Green lived upstairs. Although not luxurious it was more spacious and less spartan than what they'd been used to at Hammersmith Terrace.

Only a few feet of riverside pathway separates Ship House, as 56 Strand-on-the-Green is now called, from the river. At high tide the river washes close by. In fact the front door is built several feet above the level of the path, presumably as a flood precaution. Lewis and his wife occupied the small cottage in the garden, the same cottage which was, many years later, briefly occupied by Dylan Thomas. There is a gate in the property's boundary wall which gives access to a footpath running at right angles to the river. From the gate it is only a few paces to Thames Road. Green's timber was, presumably, delivered along Thames Road by dray and carried into the workshop through the gate.

Green was now well-placed, about mid-way between Kew's road and rail bridges, to take to the water again, mostly in a half-decked 20-foot sharpie, *The Tomboy*. It was made of half-inch wood and designed for rowing by boys in calm water. Green added an iron plate to *The Tomboy* to strengthen her for sailing, but nonetheless always felt that she was in imminent danger of breaking in half if she pitched in steep seas under full sail. Spencer and Spink, influenced by Green, soon equipped themselves with a 12-foot dinghy and the four of them often sailed upstream or downstream of the nearby bridges on the Thames.

Strand-on-the-Green

They also took off down-river at weekends. The whole of London with all its bridges and traffic lay between them and the open sea. Nothing daunted, they would head for Holehaven Creek where it joins the Thames at Canvey Island, or further east to Southend and beyond. Sometimes they headed south for the Medway estuary and Kent, calling at Sheerness and Queenborough on the Isle of Sheppey or at Cliffe on the Hoo peninsula.

Such intrepid sailing was (is?) unusual on the Thames and Green found it challenging because *The Tomboy* often had to lower her sail, and sometimes her mast, to get under the first dozen or so of the eighteen bridges. Then he had to shoot the wider bridges 'head to wind', sometimes on the point of meeting, or being overtaken by, a tug with a string of barges. Below the bridges conditions were often choppy and potentially dangerous, given the craft Green was sailing in. But how he loved it. These lines describe boating in 1913, 'In the year before the fatal year':

.... We came once more to Maldon town
Now from the sea on which before we look'd so gladly down
And even as our sails were spread upon the silver streak
The winding estuary branc'd with many a fairy creek.

Sometimes they left the Thames and explored the Grand Union Canal as far as Tring, breaking ice as they went if it was winter time. He loved the gaily decorated barges and the 'rude engineering' of the locks which they encountered on their way. He was also always attracted by the old arched bridges because he loathed 'modern contraptions' of concrete or iron.

There was some boat building in the workshop too. Green received his first order at Strand-on-the-Green from a minor novelist, Alfred Oliphant. Oliphant died before the boat was finished but it was bought jointly by Richard Mather and his sailing partner. Green also built a small sharpie, just for rowing, for the artist Frederick Carter.

Mather - later managing Director of Skinninggrove Iron Company in Cleveland and very prosperous - was a young, newly-married man living in Blackheath when Green first met him. He and his wife, Marie, ordered a set of dining room furniture from Green, including one of his innovative draw tables, in spite of the Mathers not being well off at this time. Later they bought a house in Dulwich which Green was commissioned to furnish throughout, the only complete house he ever did.

54

Chair which converts into a table.
Made for Richard and Marie Mather by Arthur Romney Green.

Mather is a good example of Green's dictum that you cannot successfully make customers out of your friends, but you can certainly make wonderful friends out of your customers. Mather and his family became close friends. Green and Bertha dined at Blackheath - where sometimes the Mathers could only afford to eat pickled herrings. Green was to be godfather to the Mathers' son John Romney.

Another of the new, lasting, friends Green and Bertha made at Strand-on-the-Green was Francis Macnamara, a striking Irishman and poet, who had turned his back on the family estates in the west of Ireland and brought his wife to live in London. One of his children, Caitlin, would later marry Dylan Thomas, long after Caitlin's mother, Yvonne, had parted from the father of her children and embarked on a long lesbian love affair.

Macnamara was an individualist who, in Green's words, 'toyed with the subject of money reform but could never at any time abide grousing in prose or verse whether in personal or social matters.' Green admired Macnamara's verse and he and Spencer persuaded Macnamara to read his poetry several times at their Sunday Evening Circle.

Macnamara was a friend of Augustus John and introduced Bertha to John in the hope that John would be instantly captivated by her so that he would paint her. John didn't take the bait, to Green's disappointment, although she was later drawn by Eric Gill.

56 Strand-on-the-Green in modern times.

Gill and his wife, Mary, also visited Green and Bertha at Strand-on the-Green and the two men enjoyed some sailing together. One year, like two schoolboys on an adventure, they camped out afloat on Christmas Eve, enjoying a long evening and a comfortable night in the cabin which they heated by means of a toaster on a primus stove.

Writing continued as usual, alongside some half-hearted involvement with the newly formed Hammersmith Branch of the National Guilds League (NGL), although Green was too much his 'own man' ever to remain committed to any form of socialism for long because he always disagreed with individuals on specific points. He was never one to adopt pre-packed philosophies.

The free-thinking Herbert Reiach, to whom he was introduced by a yachtsman who observed a daring sailing feat by Green in the Thames estuary, published a number of Green's articles - and some poems - in *Yachting Monthly* which had been founded in 1906. These included a socialist-patriotic 'verse-pamphlet', admired by Eric Gill, in early 1915. Unfortunately it then had to be withdrawn because the 'Censor' was disturbed by it.

In 1912 Green wrote a series of five well-paid and beautifully produced articles for *Burlington Magazine*, edited by Roger Fry, by now a well known artist and art critic - and an old friend of Bertha's. In these pieces he developed an argument that art is a symptom of social disease. Green was pleased, three or four years later, to attend a series of lectures given by Bertrand Russell and to find Russell pursuing a similar line - although Green could not for himself accept Russell's extreme pacifist stance.

Green was 42 when war was declared in August 1914 and too old to volunteer. By the time conscription began later in the war Green was in his mid-forties and unfit. Although, as he remarked wryly, given the colossal loss of life and the need for new 'blood', he certainly wouldn't have been thought too old by the end of the war. He felt later that people of his generation who hadn't served in the 'Great' war had, in a sense, a dimension missing.

He wasn't a conscientious objector, although his thoughtful attitude towards war - both in 1914 and 1939 - has often been misunderstood. Resident in Durban at the outbreak of the Boer War, he was quite annoyed that teachers were not permitted to enlist - because otherwise he would have done so.

In 1914 he was critical of conscientious objectors. You cannot reasonably object to something whose inherited advantages you are enjoying, he felt.

In other words, for centuries Britain has enriched herself by fighting and winning many wars overseas - and every Briton is a beneficiary of that. He also believed that there are more important and fundamental things to object to than war: Industrialisation and what he saw as its consequent totality of man's exploitation by man. This poem sums up his position.

Pacifism

Let us exploit in different places
The white, the black and yellow races,
But do not let us have the bother
And fuss of fighting with one another
So they exclaim'd, and hearken'd even
  As though it were a voice from heaven
  Whilst their new Angel pointed out,
  Beyond a shadow of a doubt,
  That since war clearly cannot pay,
  The Traders' Peace has come to stay
  There may be peace, he quite believes,
  As well as honour amongst the thieves.
  Let's wallow in the Traders' Peace
  And on our wicked navies cease
  To waste the cash which we then hope
  You'll spend on chocolate and on soap . . .
  A great illusion 'tis that war
  Pays, maybe, but a greater far
  Is that it pays, you solemn asses
    To prey upon the working classes:
    Of which I trust, in season due
    This war will disillusion you:
    And cost what millions then it may
    One war will have been made to pay.

Green's bit for the war effort was to manufacture aeroplane propellers in late 1914 and during 1915 under the auspices of Sir Charles Allom. By then, Lewis was dead and his successor, Thompson, in the army - so the workshop was far from busy. And notwithstanding the war, he and Bertha were beginning to find their huge circle of friends in London oppressive. They hankered for something quieter. It wasn't therefore too much of a blow, after Green had struggled out of a third serious bout of bronchitis within as many years, to be told by his doctors in 1915 that he needed to move out of London for the benefit of his health. He was actually diagnosed at this point - presumably wrongly - as being tubercular like his father.

Some of the furniture made for Richard and Marie Mather.

Before he and Bertha finally left London, Green spent a three-week convalescent holiday with his mother in a seaside cottage owned by his sister Margaret at Pett, between Winchelsea and Hastings on the Sussex coast. From there they could hear the guns booming across the Channel in France. While Green was perforce resting, Bertha, assisted by the last retainer, Harrison, and by Gertrude Spink, wound up the workshop at Strand-on-the-Green.

Now what to do and where to go? As so often before Green fell back on his original profession and applied for a teaching job. Far from 'giving up teaching', as it has often been said that he did, Green was now to teach continuously, and mostly full-time, from 1916 until 1928. He and Bertha spent two happy terms at Abbotsholme, a school which still exists, near Uttoxeter in Staffordshire. In Green's time Dr Cecil Reddie was headmaster.

Green always had trenchant - curiously modern and free-thinking - views about education, believing that the ubiquitous, examination-driven, curriculum was generally narrow, dull and utilitarian. He approved hugely, therefore, of the short-lived experiment being conducted at Abbotsholme under Reddie in which none of the boys was entered for any kind of exam. So Green had a free hand with the curriculum and he taught the boys how to construct cardboard sundials.

He and Bertha lived in a cottage and ate their meals communally. Bertha enjoyed Reddie's company because he was a good musician. She also liked the unconventional chapel services and, out of school hours, she and Green explored the beauties of Staffordshire and Derbyshire, on bicycles and on foot.

But Bertha - the antithesis of Florence - believed in her Romney, primarily as a craftsman. She thought he was wasted as a teacher. Abbotsholme was therefore only a temporary interlude while they found some way of setting up a workshop once more.

During their Christmas holiday from Abbotsholme they found a cottage to rent at West Mersea, on the Thames estuary in south Essex - a yachtsman's paradise with which they were already familiar from their sailing trips down the Thames. They sent some of their furniture to West Mersea and were then joined there by the old workman, Harrison, who had formerly worked for Green in London but was too old to have been taken by the war.

For the next three years, with Harrison's help, Green was able to keep his 'little business' just ticking over at West Mersea - but of course it didn't pay enough to live on. He therefore had to continue teaching. And there were plenty of jobs to choose from, since most able-bodied men were away because of the war. He took a post at Bournemouth. He and Bertha lived in 'diggins' near the school during term time and travelled 'home' to West Mersea during the school holidays, except for the summer term of 1919 when, because Bertha had been ill for a long period before Easter, he left her at West Mersea for thirteen week's convalescence.

At West Mersea Green made, among other items, some elaborate inlaid triptychs. Assisted by Harrison, in 1918 he also made a refectory table of brown oak for the Mairets - whose house, 'Gospels' at Ditchling, was now finished.

Also in 1918 Green collaborated with Eric Gill in a delightful little book *Woodwork in Principle and Practice*, published by Pepler's St Dominic's Press at Ditchling. Green wrote the text and Gill provided the illustrations. Because this was a limited edition it has become a collector's item and there are very few copies of it around now. There is one, however, on display in the Hilary Bourne Gallery at Ditchling Museum. Green's contribution was volume 1 of a three-part work. Gill later wrote the text for the second volume and Mairet for the third.

Green and Bertha found Bournemouth - by then a fashionable watering place - rather dull, although they enjoyed cycling along the coast in both directions at weekends. It was on one of these trips that they found, at Christchurch, the premises in which they were to settle for the rest of their lives.

Chapter 7: A Christchurch Workshop in the 1920s

An old Victorian grocer's shop, 25 Bridge Street, lay a few yards over the Avon Bridge heading out of Christchurch in what was then Hampshire. With the river so close and the muddy creek running down to the Avon along the back of Green's and other properties, he effectively had river access just as he had had at Strand-on-the-Green. Although the creek sometimes dried out in summer, for much of the time Green could, and did, swim or sail away from the bottom of his own garden into the Avon, past its confluence with the Stour and towards the open sea. Conversely, sometimes at high tide and/or in very wet weather, the garden and back of the house was flooded. He described his beloved home thus:

And so we come by an old-world street, through a modern thoroughfare'
To our river-skirted home in the poignant borderland;
Past whose ancient front the tide of painted automobiles flows in fury,
But whose posterns open to the cry of redshank,
Hyacinths beneath the mulberry
And the music of the flight of the swan.

Today the geography is different. Bridge Street was re-numbered in the 1930s and the French restaurant which now occupies Green's former premises, and sports a commemorative blue plaque, is No.3. The back garden behind it is quite short, the creek has been filled in and there are newish buildings behind. Christchurch Marina, built after Green's time, has altered the views. And since local government reorganisation in 1974 Christchurch has found itself in Dorset.

The property had been empty for three years and was very run down in 1919 when Green and Bertha found it. It was probably also therefore very cheap - because it's not at all clear how he paid for it. Having worked as a teacher for nearly four years he may have accrued some savings. He could have taken some kind of bank loan or mortgage on the strength of his steady, if modest, schoolmaster's salary. It is, however, most likely that Green had some kind of help from his brother William, although there is no evidence of this.

25 Bridge Street had two large shop rooms at street level, with bow windows only separated by a narrow pavement from the London-bound, pre-bypass, traffic out of Christchurch. At the back was a long, overgrown, but 'nice old' garden with a mulberry tree at the bottom near the creek, as well as other fruit trees. Green soon converted an old apple loft in the garden into an outside workshop to house four work benches.

There were several upper rooms, the largest of which was at the front. Green and Bertha used it as a bedroom. From there they looked across what Green described as a 'roaring thoroughfare' into a butcher's shop and an old post office.

Green thought the rear view from the spare bedroom and from his 'den' was one of the loveliest in England. He could see the boats and the birds on the river as well as the calm dignity of Christchurch Priory - 'more nearly a cathedral but not so called.' He loved the symmetry of the five arches of the nearby bridge, describing the built arch 'so gracefully suspended over empty space by virtue of its own weight' as one of the miracles of human art like the sailing ship and the bicycle.

They moved in during the school holidays in August 1919 and immediately began to establish a workshop which would function during the day while Green continued to teach. Harrison moved to Christchurch with them from West Mersea and was Green's first foreman there. Soon there was a staff of eight to ten men and boys constructing to Green's designs, and occasionally to his brother's, at 25 Bridge Street.

When Green took over 25 Bridge Street its only sanitation was what Graham Castle describes as a 'midden' in the garden. Inevitably, it wasn't long before Green was compelled by the authorities to install adequate sanitation for all the people using the premises. This he did - with a certain amount of wryly amused resentment. Two flush lavatories, one for the men and another for Green and Bertha, were put in the back of the building. Only Green, lover of 'rural hygiene' and forward-thinking environmentalist, would then pen a sonnet 'To a Water Closet'. And he isn't really joking.

> How hath the nation been deceived in thee,
> Vile trap, preposterous mouth-piece of the hold
> Of hell! O, what the labour and the gold
> Lost to procure this deadlier loss! - to be,
> With earth's rich nutriment of field and tree,
> Her fruits ungrown, ungather'd, suck'd and roll'd
> Through subterranean arteries manifold,
> And down polluted river to the sea:
>
> The sea, once blue, now foul'd, on which our sway
> Declines, our fields, once green on which it grew,
> Grimed by black arts already in decay,
> Our millions herded to the Pit by you,
> And all they loved and lived by stolen away,
> And foul'd or famish'd all that's green and blue.

The right-hand shop, nearest to the Avon Bridge, was the low-ceilinged workshop containing several work benches. Green liked the fact that passers-by could look through the window and watch the work in progress, some of which went on in here and some in the converted apple loft outside. Finished items were displayed in the left-hand shop which served for many years as Green's showroom. Some of the heavy work was done in a converted tool shed which the men called the 'orticle' shed because it contained such 'orticles' as a circular saw and a band saw, driven by hand or foot power.

Green professed to have no theoretical objection to the use of machinery 'if it can be made to pay without detriment to the quality of the work.' But he was temperamentally opposed to it. Not only did he enjoy the healthy hard work of planing and sawing but he thought it was important that all his men should be allowed to 'do their bit imparting something of the beauty of nature to the work of their hands.' However, for what would now be called 'health and safety' reasons, coupled with economy, he usually got his exceptionally heavy sawing and planing done at the local sawmill.

Of course in these post-war years there were plenty of young, and older, men seeking jobs and new beginnings. The workshop rapidly became a full and busy place where Green was universally addressed and referred to by his initials 'A.R.G.' Harrison, who was quite elderly and given to drinking, had, with reluctance on Green's part, to be eased out after about two years. Arthur Terry - shell shocked after the war and in debt - then joined Green from Haslemere with his rather unsatisfactory son, Norman. Terry took over as headman.

Green also engaged Londoners Alfred Eades, who had worked for him before the war, and his brother Tom. Romer Chattock, who was ex-public school and who came from a prosperous family, worked as 'odd job man'. Christchurch had a fund for the payment of moderate apprenticeship premiums, so Green was never short of good apprentices. Leslie Edney from Purewell, for example.

Robin Nance, who went on to establish his own well-known designer-woodworker business in St Ives in Cornwall, also trained for three years under Green during the 1920s. 'I being quite numberless there was probably not much hope of his [Green's] communicating ideas about design to me,' recalled Nance. 'I once drew the lines of the Cutty Sark by algebraic formulae under his instructions . . . his treatment of us boys, in his withdrawn way, was most tolerant . . I must say what a generous man A.R.G. was, though I wonder if he knew it.'

The Christchurch Workshop, workers from left to right: Leslie Edney, Robin Nance, Alfred Eades, Arthur Romney Green, Eric Sharpe, William Merritt, Samuel Dann, Graham Castle and Romer Chattock.

William Merritt, a Christchurch man who was a year or two older than Norman Terry and infinitely more competent, was taken on in 1921. Merritt, who eventually became Green's foreman, was later described in a testimonial given him by Green as 'trustworthy and industrious' as well as 'the best all round woodworker I have ever employed.'

Graham Castle was 15 when he began his apprenticeship with Green in 1925. Graham's brother Edgar, five years younger, later followed in his footsteps. Sadly, of course, Green couldn't take on everyone who approached him and recorded having to send a boy and his mother away in tears because he simply had no room for another apprentice. Green usually employed what he called 'a semi-imbecile' to sweep up and do simple jobs as a means of giving work to a 'bottom-dog' who wouldn't otherwise have had any.

Stanley Webb Davies, then aged 26, joined Green in 1920. Davies had come from a wealthy Lancashire mill owning family and Bertha admired him very much for turning his back on factory management. After war service in the Friends' War Victims Relief Unit, dubbed the 'War Vics' for short, and a brief spell in the cotton mill which clearly put him off, Davies decided to devote the rest of his life to woodwork, along the lines of Morris and Ruskin.

Like Nance, Davies spent three years at Christchurch before setting up on his own. A house and a workshop were built for him, with financial help from his father, at Windermere in 1926. Green and Bertha were later to spend some happy holidays at Windermere with Davies and his wife, Emily.

In 1967 Davies wrote his memories of the Christchurch workshop and of Green, whom he described as 'an exceptional man, of strong but balanced opinions, an original thinker and designer, a poet, a mathematician and a hater of humbug.'

Davies continued: 'My eyes were opened to a new and thrilling experience of the furniture maker's art and I fell in love with the work I saw. . . His premises were in contrast to the loveliness of the work that was produced . . . He gathered round him a medley of craftsmen in differing crafts and of varying abilities as well as pupils, some working quite independently to give a helping hand when needed. . . At that time to be associated with Green was an education, inspiration, enlightenment and joy where something new was ever arising.' In 1974 Stanley Davies remarked 'In retrospect I almost worship Romney Green. I can recall now the thrill at first seeing his work.'

Eric Sharpe, Bedales-educated and having served in the Artists' Rifles, joined Green's workshop in 1921 and stayed for eight years. He was a superb carver as well as a cabinet maker and designer in his own right. 'Sharpe achieved interesting and impressive designs by means of the method of construction he employed,' recorded Davies. 'And he produced some of the most original and splendid pieces especially in chairs, developed from the same sound woodwork tradition followed by Green and yet quite different from Green's work. I do not think that Sharpe's unique method of carving, in connection with his independent sculpture in the round, all of which gave him immense pleasure, owed anything to Green's influence.'

It is hardly surprising therefore that two such different men as Green and Sharpe didn't always see eye-to-eye. It was a quarrel with Green which eventually precipitated Sharpe's removal to Martyr Worthy, near Winchester, where he established his own workshop and home in 1930. Graham Castle, who remembers that both men smoked large smelly pipes of Hampshire tobacco, doesn't recall the exact cause of the final dispute because 'there was usually some sort of disagreement going on between them.'

Nonetheless, in later life both Green and Sharpe were carefully respectful of each other's abilities and achievements. Writing many years later Sharpe referred to Green as 'that grand old man of English woodwork' and commented that 'Eight years arguing principles with him would cure anyone of crankiness!' He went on to recall that 'He [Green] never ran down other people's things because he thought they were good and might be competitive. But he was just as delighted as if he had done them himself and you cannot pretend that Romney Green could afford competition.' Green was full of praise for Sharpe's carving and recorded that Sharpe had very good reason not to regard himself as a 'pupil' during his eight years at Christchurch.

If an order was for a set of chairs Green always made the first one himself until he was satisfied with it. Then the rest could be made by the men. There was never any batch production. Once a man was assigned to a job, Graham Castle explains, he saw it right through to the end, so that he had a real sense of 'ownership' in the item. Totally opposed to the economics and 'slavery' of the factory floor, Green wanted each man to have the experience of making something beautiful.

The men were paid punctiliously. 'You never had to ask Green for money and no one ever asked him for a rise,' says Graham Castle. 'He paid everyone what they were worth with scrupulous fairness. And if you wanted to do a job on your own in the workshop after hours that was fine, but he'd make a tiny hourly charge for the use of the light to keep everything straight.'

Green was very open about his financial affairs. Stanley Davies described the quarterly 'company' meetings which were held in an upstairs room. 'All associated with the place would meet and Green would show us the books and tell us how much he himself expected to gain from the work of each man and pupil. I believe he would have liked to start a profit sharing scheme but profits were not large enough to warrant it.'

Trade was brisk and the workshop kept very lively during most of the 1920s. Green believed that he was advantaged by being based in a beauty spot because he often attracted interest from passing visitors. Local householders also bought a lot of furniture - beds, cupboards, cabinets, chests, tables and chairs - as well as smaller items, many of which are probably still sitting, well-used, in the homes of ordinary individuals who don't recognise a solid functional piece which has been in the family for three generations as being anything special. The dining room suite, with its inimitable geometric patterning, now displayed in Christchurch's Red House Museum, is a good example of Green's household work.

Some pieces were made for stock and for display in the showroom. Anyone who wanted to buy could either take a stock item or commission a similar one, perhaps in a different wood. Oak, chestnut and walnut were the most usual, although Green occasionally used important timbers such as mahogany for special orders.

Many clients came from further afield. Richard Mather continued to be a dear friend and good customer. So was Mr Richard B. Wright of Michelham Priory, Sussex. Wright had original design ideas of his own and he and Green worked out together exactly what was required.

Eric Gill commissioned for Pigotts, his home at High Wycombe, a 15-foot long and 10-foot high display piece, which Green designed especially. Graham Castle was involved in its making and recalls that the chestnut had to be bought in specially. Robert Speaight's 1966 biography of Gill describes the Gills' living room as 'long and spacious, and the entire side of the southern wall was taken up by a huge dresser made by Romney Green and bright with pewter plates. . .' The cabinet was later inherited by Gill's daughter, Joan Hague, who took it to her home in Ireland. It was finally sold, after Joan's death, to an unknown customer by a London company in the early 1980s.

Items, made by A.R.G., with characteristic geometrical patterning.

Green did some work for Charterhouse, the boys' independent school near Godalming in Surrey, including the big oak refectory table for Hodgsonites house, a photograph of which he used for advertising purposes. Then there was a table for Christchurch Sailing Club and the choir stalls for the parish church at Mudeford. Graham Castle remembers that for protection of furniture in transit Green ingeniously used a strip of wet fur round the top of the packing case, which prevented the lid blowing off.

Eric Gill procured for Green an important order for a war memorial lychgate at Catherington Church, between Havant and Petersfield. 'Inside' the gate, designed into the pleasing geometrical shape of the construction, are four rectangular panels on which are carved the names of the dead. According to Graham Castle it was from Gill that Green learned how to cut letters. Each panel is edged with Green's characteristic fine-lined diamond patterning. The structure includes elegantly angled shelves on which - to this day - Catherington families place wreaths.

Author at the memorial lychgate, All Saints Church, Catherington, Hants.

Inside the memorial lychgate.

Still not a member of the Arts and Crafts Exhibition Society, Green nonetheless exhibited two items at the 13th exhibition held at the Royal Academy, Burlington House in 1926. These were a table in English walnut at £ 6-16-6d (£6.82) and a wardrobe of English walnut at £42-10-0 (£42.50). By 1928 Green had been elected a member of the Society and, at the 14th exhibition, he showed an armchair in walnut, on which he and Sharpe had both worked and for which Edmund Hunter had provided a tapestry seat. Its price was £14-14-0 (£14.70).

He was also exhibiting locally in the 1920s. The eighth exhibition of the Bournemouth Arts Club held in the Dalkeith Studio, Old Christchurch Road, over the 1927/8 Christmas-New Year period mentions a walnut armchair at £10-0-0 and an invalid tea tray at £5-5-0 (£5.25), both by Green, along with six items by Sharpe. Further afield, Green also exhibited pieces at the Liverpool Autumn exhibitions held at Walker Art Gallery in 1927, 1928 and 1929.

In 1928 Green's *Instead of a Catalogue* was printed by St Dominic's Press, Ditchling and published by New Handworkers' Gallery, 14 Percy Street, London W1. It commemorated his first 25 years as a woodworker and describes his attitude to work, what he makes and how the pieces are constructed. The booklet is a statement of position and an oblique advertisement. You cannot catalogue anything which is worth having he argues.

He explains his hatred of mixed materials: 'Furniture should be made of wood with the least possible mixture of any other material. The telescope table with its great iron screw, and the modern bedstead with its garish ends miraculously supported by its ugly invisible side irons are spoiled to my mind, just as much as modern architecture is spoiled by a too extensive use of iron.'

He goes on to describe the sorts of things which his workshop produced, such as 'easy chairs with backs adjustable on knuckle joint hinges and extending leg rests, which are thus as comfortable as a good sofa though the elegance of the woodwork is not smothered in upholstery.'

Then he mentions 'roll top writing tables, not of lath and canvas in the yellow utilitarian style, but framed and panelled in figured walnut or mahogany, which rise automatically and recede into a space evacuated only just in time by pigeon holes as the desk is drawn forward.' One thinks of the delightful knee hole desk which Green gave his niece, William's daughter Joan, as a twenty-first birthday gift. She was 21 in the year that *Instead of a Catalogue* was published. Her desk is still in the family.

As soon as he had settled in at Christchurch, Green wanted to build boats commercially. Knowing this, his brother financed the building of a sixteen foot dinghy *Triolet*. The idea was that sailing club members would see her and be sufficiently impressed to place orders. As a strategy it failed. Green blamed this on the fact that he had given *Triolet* a rather strange new triplane rig, invented by Percy Tatchell, although Green won several races in her.

Once he had invented his innovative method of geometrical design which gave him an exact way of calculating the stresses, there were some orders for boats, mostly executed by Alfred Eades and later by Edgar Castle who became a fine boat builder. In the 1928 Christchurch town guide Green advertised himself as 'Woodworker and Boat Builder' and his letterheads from about the same date say 'Designer Woodworker and Boatbuilder - Fair hulls produced by geometrical methods.'

A. ROMNEY GREEN, 3 BRIDGE STREET, CHRISTCHURCH, HANTS.

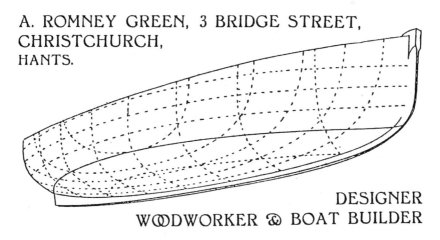

DESIGNER WOODWORKER & BOAT BUILDER

Graham Castle remembers a boat which was made for Lord Rothermere and which had to be delivered to a larger vessel in Mudeford Harbour while the tide was right. None of the lads was keen to do the rowing. They preferred to rest against a breakwater on the beach after a day's work. Green coughed and set off in it himself. He came back with a £5-0-0 'tip' for safe delivery. Instead of pocketing it and castigating his lazy employees, he sent them to buy some cheese and other food with some beer so that they could all enjoy a little party. 'A generous man indeed,' as Robin Nance observed.

Being a member of Green's Christchurch workshop in its heyday was more of a way of life than a job. Davies remembered with excitement that upstairs was a 'small cramped and cosy little living room, with a south view over the river, harbour, ancient priory and distant headland, filled with furniture of his own making. It was the setting for many exciting Sunday evening readings and discussions, over coffee, with visiting fellow craftsmen, artists, poets, social reformers and forward looking people. Of course Green knew Francis Macnamara, Philip Mairet and Hilary Pepler. It was probably these, and others like them, that Davies recalled. Graham Castle also has fond and grateful memories of the sense of community, shared interests and ongoing education engendered by those Sunday evenings.

Bertha, meanwhile, was lovingly supporting Green and his business. She continued in the 'housework' that she was so good at, although she did at this time have help - both indoors and outdoors in the garden which had to be retrieved from its overgrown state when they first moved into 25 Bridge Street. Soon Green was able to grow in the garden the asparagus of which he was so fond.

Ever determined to do what she could to increase their income, Bertha did a little teaching. Philip Baker, who was born in 1917 and whose parents knew Green, remembers coming to her for lessons with his brother in an upstairs room at the back of the house when he was about seven or eight. He recalls that the only way in was through the workshop which was always deep in woodshavings. 'Green seemed an aloof figure who took little notice of the arriving children,' he recalls.

The men adored Bertha. Graham Castle remembers that she always joined them for tea breaks in the workshop. She provided the milk for their tea and shared the afternoon cake for which one of the lads - often Romer Chattock - popped out and bought from a local shop. She was interested in what they were doing and she knew them all well. Naturally she joined them in the Sunday evening sessions too.

She and Green were still unmarried, and although most of their London friends had been aware of their position, they saw little need to advertise it on arrival in Christchurch. When, however, the Vicar of Christchurch, Canon Gay, decided to order some pieces for the Lady Chapel in the Priory, Green thought that he had better 'own up'. And his honesty cost him the order. It wasn't until several years later, when Gay's successor saw Green's and Bertha's dog, Fanny, clad in a cosy jacket, that he observed that a man who looked after his dog so well couldn't be all bad, so he placed an order.

Prayer desk, Christchurch Priory.

Consequently there are two lovely prayer desks in the Lady Chapel. Instead of a ball shape for the hand to grasp at the top of each upright, there is a truncated octahedron. It's a mathematical idea typical to Green. He had the same shape carved in stone for eventual use on his tombstone. Also in the Priory are two moveable altar rails and a magnificent ceremonial chair.

Ceremonial chair, Christchurch Priory.

75

Moveable altar rails, Christchurch Priory, showing details of carving.

And all this time Green continued to teach full-time. He worked in what would now be called a 'peripatetic' way - cycling to schools from Poole in one direction and to New Milton in the other. He would do just a couple of hours or a half-day in each. He did this until the end of 1927 and had written a text book entitled *Mathematics Made Interesting*, in three volumes, for which he was unable to find a publisher.

It was at one of his schools - a girls' establishment - that the pupils asked him to define the object of education. In response he coined what has become almost a Green catch-phrase saying: 'The objects of life are to do adventurous things, to make (or at all events enjoy) beautiful things, to understand wonderful things.'

Then, after nearly 19 years of separation, his wife Florence decided to divorce him. She and her old flame from Durban were considering marriage so she wanted to be free - although, in the event, she didn't remarry. Local people read in the newspapers that Green was being divorced and assumed, not unreasonably, that Bertha was the instigator. The ensuing misunderstanding and 'scandal' caused Green some problems - especially when he then immediately married the woman they had long assumed to be his wife. It then made his position as a teacher untenable.

Romney Green and Bertha Murray were married at the Register Office in the district of Bournemouth and Christchurch on 2nd February 1928. Trelawney Dayrell-Reed and Vere Bartrick Baker were witnesses. The new Mr and Mrs Romney Green had been in love for 25 years and had lived together for 19. It thereafter became a family joke - which Green used to tell against himself with his characteristic shouts of laughter: 'And the only time in my whole life I did the right thing I got the sack for it!'

Chapter 8: Beyond the Workshop

Although Green enjoyed living the whole of his full and active life 'to the lees', the 1920s was probably the best, busiest and happiest decade of all. The workshop was flourishing, at least until the onset of national economic depression towards the end of the decade. Because he also had a teaching income there was a reasonable amount of money for him and Bertha to live on.

In spite of her nascent heart trouble Bertha was still in good health. They were in a place they adored and were able to do together most of the things they liked doing. Green was no longer a young man; his fiftieth birthday fell in 1922. Yet when you consider how much he managed to achieve in the 1920s, in addition to running the workshop and teaching full-time, you begin to realise what an exceptionally energetic and creative man he was.

Bertha with their sheepdog, Fanny.

Poetry poured out of him. In 1926 he had published by Allen and Unwin a delightful little book *Twenty-One Sonnets* which was favourably reviewed in the *Times Literary Supplement*. It was a limited edition of 300 copies, of which 250 were for sale. It included 'Tree-Worship at the Bench', 'Green Places' and 'To a Water Closet', along with a lovely one entitled 'To her sheepdog in my wife's absence' which must have been written when Bertha was, for some reason, temporarily away from home and much missed by both man and dog.

The dog, Fanny, was given to them as a puppy by Trelawney Dayrell-Reed in the spring of 1924. She was long-haired and cream-coloured and she lived for a remarkable 16 years, until 1940. Both Green and Bertha were very fond of Fanny who was assiduously brushed daily by Bertha for 10 years. 'Wife' is a courtesy title for Bertha at this date.

> Poor lass, our light's gone out, for she's away:
>   And here we are, each with our second best
>   Comrade, in this so dear forsaken nest
> To mourn her loss - she at whose side all day,
> The shadow of my Love, you rose or lay,
>   Bounded or slept: the glory and the zest
> Of life are founder'd in our ceaseless quest
> For that light-bearing presence gone astray.
>
> O grey enquiring muzzle, pleading eyes,
>   And lifted paw - O worshipper devout
> Of empty slippers, searcher in such sad wise
>   Of empty rooms - O wanderer about
> Deserted bed, where not a flower but sighs
>   With you and me - How has our light gone out!

Twenty-One Sonnets was published under the pseudonym 'J.S.N.' This was because Green felt that the sonnets 'Reprieve', which celebrates Beatrice's reappearance in his life and 'Love and Death', a passionate and quite erotic love poem to Bertha, revealed the truth of his marital history and could therefore be an embarrassment to him as a teacher. Afterwards he regretted this decision because the book sold disappointingly few copies. He believed it would have done much better had his identity as its author been known. He also thought that his girl pupils would surely have been intrigued enough to buy his book - thereby increasing sales - if they had known that their teacher had written it. And none of it made any difference to his teaching career anyway because, as things turned out, he had to resign shortly after the publication of *Twenty-One Sonnets* when news of his impending divorce broke.

The brilliant, charismatic, but unreliable, Francis Macnamara moved to Christchurch soon after Green and Bertha did. He lived on a houseboat on the river and tried, unsuccessfully, to scratch a living as a private tutor. One of his pupils was Augustus John's son, Romilly, who wrote a biography at the age of 25. Macnamara was now 'on' his second of three wives and Green felt quite flattered that he flirted 'vainly but outrageously' with Bertha.

Green admired Macnamara very much, in spite of - or perhaps because of - Macnamara's individualist, fickle behaviour. Green genuinely valued Macnamara's fierce criticism of his poems. Augustus John, who had a house at Poole, would often turn up in Christchurch for 'Bohemian' drinking sessions with Macnamara. Green may have got to know John better at this time. It is also quite likely that John attended some of Green's Sunday evening meetings - although there is no evidence for this.

It was Macnamara who introduced Green to Trelawney Dayrell-Reed. Dayrell-Reed was an artist, poet and farmer who lived just across the county boundary in Dorset. Together the three men formed the Christchurch Poetry Society. At first they used Green's rooms, but as interest grew they needed larger accommodation and took to meeting in hired public halls, in pubs and elsewhere.

The society launched the quarterly *Wessex Review* and paid Macnamara 'a generous salary' to act as editor, but it took him a year to bring out the first issue - which included nothing by Green - by which time the society was bankrupted. Then Macnamara left Christchurch for his native Ireland, having resolved his family quarrel there. Green recounts this with wry amusement and no shred of resentment. The second and last issue of *Wessex Review* was financed and edited by Rev. A.D.H. Allen, Headmaster of Wimborne Grammar School.

When Macnamara left, Lawrence Housman, playwright, author, critic and biographer brother of the more famous A (Alfred) E (Edward), took over as president of the Christchurch Poetry Society. Under his leadership for five or six years the society brought out an annual anthology of local work, each containing 30 poems by different hands. Dayrell-Reed, Margaret Eyres, Green's old friend Percival Strong and, of course, Green himself were amongst the regular contributors. Green thought that the quality of these anthologies would have justified publication in a good London journal.

Because several key people moved away the Poetry Society began to flag after a few years and so it was disbanded. But Green, of course, went on writing poems. *Wessex* (not to be confused with *Wessex Review*) claimed to be an 'annual record of the movement for a university of Wessex based on University College Southampton.' It was first published in 1928. In it, alongside poems by Robert Bridges and Siegfried Sassoon, and contributions from Macnamara, Dayrell-Reed and Lawrence Housman, are six poems by A. Romney Green. The 1929 issue of *Wessex* advertises a forthcoming sonnet competition with a prize of 1 guinea. Lawrence Housman was the judge and he awarded the prize to Green's sonnet 'Quaestio' - the title is a Latin noun which means seeking, searching or inquiry. Later Green renamed it 'The Adventurer'.

> The hints of God, the hints of power malign -
> The sunset here, and there Vesuvius glows!
> Cyclone and canker, June and the wild rose,
> Cockroach and viper, apricot and vine -
> Portents diverse, but no conclusive sign!
> The soul of man, a will o' the wisp that shows
> And fades above the foetal slime, who knows,
> Of deathless hung in firmaments divine?
>
> Who knows, and would not even prefer
> Such boundary set to knowledge - not be sad
> If no such undiscover'd land there were
> Beyond the charted paradise, no mad
> Terror, and no wild hope, no thunder clad
> Horizon, and no lone adventurer.

Housman found Green's sonnet 'emotional, melodious and well thought out' and he particularly liked the third and fourth lines.

Green also wrote during the 1920s an intensely charming poem entitled 'A Strange Visit'. It consists of 11 four line verses and describes the accidental falling of a bird down his bedroom chimney: 'As down our bedroom chimney thus / The feathery scuffle and the fuss'. After Green had picked up the bird:

> His wings so delicately sown
> With black upon the velvet brown
> And, blindly quivering to be flown,
> His pulses beating to my own
>
> As, dainty feet and silver thighs
> All gather'd with smooth wings he lies
> Breast upwards and bewilder'd eyes
> A moment in my hand - and flies.

Beautifully calligraphed by Helen Hinkley 'A Strange Visit' was published as a tiny booklet in 1930 by the Pear Tree Press of Flansham, near Bognor in Sussex.

Percival Strong, who by now had a medical practice at Boston in Lincolnshire, stayed regularly with Green and Bertha at Christchurch. Bertha had become fond of Strong because he was a music lover and Green was not musical. It was at about this time that Bertha learned to play the guitar. She seems not to have had a piano at any stage after leaving California in 1901.

Not long after the collapse of the Christchurch Poetry Society, Green and Strong began to collaborate on an anthology of poetry and prose, but soon found themselves unable to agree on specifics. So they decided together that each man should prepare his own.

Green's anthology - which he wanted to call 'Eagle's Feathers' - was an eclectic collection of the writings he most admired and enjoyed. Every poem, extract or passage chosen, he wrote in his introduction, has 'memorable style or contrast'. Effectively the anthology is an account of Green's own tastes in literature. Although he would probably have detested the utilitarian notion of a literary 'canon', in fact all the great names of English literature are here: Dickens, Browning, Keats, Milton, Coleridge, Byron, Shakespeare and The Bible. Then there are the men and women that Green knew personally such as Eric Gill, Francis Macnamara, Margaret Eyres and Trelawney Dayrell-Reed. Of course his beloved Emerson and Nietzsche are there. So too are many others. As you might expect from a Romantically inclined poet like Green, Tennyson is well represented, including a passage from 'Ulysses' from which the title of this biography is taken. Green also put in a few of his own poems.

Carefully amassed during the busy 1920s, the anthology was ready for Allen and Unwin to publish in 1931. Unfortunately, and to Green's great disappointment, economic depression was by then biting hard and a crisis in paper production prevented the book's publication. It was eventually edited and abridged by Green's niece and literary executor, Joan Yeo. In 1948 Allen and Unwin published it posthumously as *A Craftsman's Anthology*.

Of course Strong was not the only visitor to stay at 25 Bridge Street. Gill and his wife stayed for a week in the early 1920s and slept in the deal double bed, painted green. Green and Bertha, he reports gleefully, meanwhile had the pleasure of sharing the narrow single bed in the spare room. Gill found Christchurch 'absurdly beautiful.'

Bertha, pencil drawing by Eric Gill.

During one visit Gill drew Bertha in pencil - to Green's delight - because he was sure that it showed that Gill could see her real loveliness. Many years later he planned to use Gill's drawings as illustrations in *Work and Play.*

Green and Gill sailed together in Green's sharpie. Green teased Gill and Mary about going to Mass to confess their sins when it meant keeping decent people waiting for their breakfast. And the two men enjoyed some heated debates during the week.

Gill had no truck with aestheticism. He didn't recognise that art - or beauty - were important for their own sake, a point of view, which Green, predictably, disputed hotly. He and Gill continued to discuss the nature of beauty and the function of art in their correspondence throughout the 1920s, as several of Gill's published letters show (*Letters of Eric Gill* Ed. Walter Shewring, Jonathan Cape 1947). After 1924 Gill was based at the remote Welsh village of Capel-y-ffin, about 14 miles north of Abergavenny.

Another visitor Green and Bertha were delighted to welcome - regularly after the first time - was his daughter, Beatrice. Having reached the age of 21 in April 1922, she was now free to make up her own mind whether to re-establish contact with her father. Graham Castle remembers that she came quite often, although she clearly had little to do with the men since, when he first discussed this with the author, he had no idea of her name or whether she was married.

Green reports that Beatrice and he became 'good friends' and that she learned to get on well with Bertha. He was especially touched that Beatrice, who remembered Bertha as a family friend at Haslemere in her childhood, told her father that she had liked Bertha even then. Macnamara flirted with her, Green records and Beatrice, probably in spite of herself, had to admit that he was an 'attractive devil.'

After university Beatrice lived in London for a while, working and speaking for the Howard League for Penal Reform. In time she married Rev. Vincent Dawkins, who was, in Green's words, 'also a mathematician and a craftsman'. So the two men had something in common. After Beatrice's marriage she and her husband visited Christchurch together from time to time. Florence, Beatrice's mother, outlived Green. Throughout this period, therefore, Beatrice must have been maintaining separate relations with both her parents. She had no children, so there are no direct Romney Green descendants.

How glad Green was to have made his peace with his daughter:

Reprieve

Wish'd for yet dreaded, whether to chastise
  Or bless, to avenge her injury or grant
  The pardon which of living things I want
From her alone, she comes, and in her eyes
Judgement suspended. It is to despise
  The traitor, or to admit the knight errant
  Even though unknightly erring? She is scant
Of words, and yet how true her heart replies.

To mine - true child of mine! - And to my Love
  Her heart replies. Refined gold she'll prove,
    Strong of two-fold loyalty to bear
    Such burthen as I bequeath'd. O Love if fear
We must, it is not vengeance from above:
  We harbour no Destroying Angel here.

Green was also pleased that, now he and Bertha were settled at Christchurch, Minnie, his mother, took to taking a two to three week holiday with them every year. Minnie - whose eightieth birthday fell in 1922 - had already got to know Bertha by visiting at Strand-on-the-Green. She was, by all accounts extraordinarily fit for her age. Graham Castle remembers that she liked to row herself around the harbour in a skiff during her annual visit, but he and the other lads had to lift her into the boat. Since Graham Castle didn't start working for Green until 1925, Minnie must have been at least 83 at the time he is recalling. They addressed her as 'Granny Green', as did Beatrice and all William's children and grandchildren. William was another regular visitor to 25 Bridge Street. Graham Castle thinks he dropped in almost weekly.

Manning Pike - 'the ablest man I ever met' - came too with his wife, Gwen. The Pikes had been friends of Green and Bertha since their earliest Hammersmith days. Pike had worked before the war as a 'manufacturer of ingenious gadgets' and between 1914 and 1918 as manager of a munitions factory. After the war he became a printer, printing T.E. Lawrence's *Seven Pillars of Wisdom* and Green's *Twenty-One Sonnets*. He and Green enjoyed sailing together in *Triolet* during Pike's visits to Christchurch. Later, alas, Green lost touch with Pike, but by chance discovered him in London many years later in the 1930s. To Green's horror and impotent anger, Pike was living in some sort of shelter for 'bottom dogs' where inmates paid their rent by chopping firewood.

A. Romney Green, Woodworker, 25, Bridge St., Christchurch

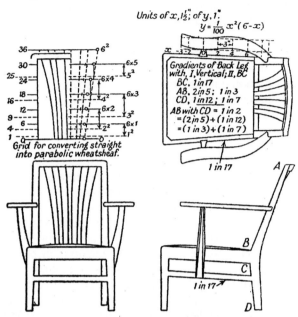

Units of x, $1\frac{1}{2}$"; of y, 1".

$$y = \frac{1}{100} x^2 (6-x)$$

Gradients of Back Leg
with, I, Vertical; II, BC
BC, 1 in 17
AB, 2 in 5; 1 in 3
CD, 1 in 12; 1 in 7
AB with CD = 1 in 2
= (2 in 5) + (1 in 12)
= (1 in 3) + (1 in 7)

1 in 17

Grid for converting straight
into parabolic wheatsheaf.

Hand-made Furniture, mainly of English-grown woods, and to original designs, from the simplest to the finest styles. Small sailing boats designed and built from solid equations. Equations found for any type of fair-bodied hull.

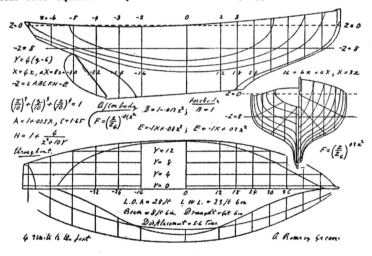

Advertisement in *Wessex*

86

As well as 'literary' work and entertaining visitors, Green wrote lectures and articles during this period. He lectured, for example, at the Christchurch Adult School. The syllabus for 1924 shows that he spoke on 'The Right Attitude to Change: The Poetry of William Morris' on 27th April and on 'How our minds work' on 29th August.

He addressed the Bournemouth Poetry Society 'In Defence of Satirical and Political Verse', telling his audience that you can hardly expect satire to be popular amongst its victims: 'politicians, minor poetasters, mandarins and tyrants, charlatans and humbugs of every degree and kind.' He was surprised, however, that satire is not more popular than it is with the general reader.

On another occasion he spoke at Bournemouth on 'Contemporary Poets and the Theory of Poetry.' He believed that however far the pendulum of poetic tastes might swing from generation to generation, there are timeless and absolute criteria by which to determine whether poetry is good or not - although no-one has ever managed to define them.

He was very damning of those he dubbed the 'Georgian' poets (he meant George V): Thomas Hardy, Robert Bridges and Walter de la Mare, because he thought that they and their readers might confuse the imaginary with the imaginative. Green regarded their poetry as fanciful rather than imaginative and without real feeling of faith in God, nature or in man.

In his lecture 'A Craftsman's Religious and Social Philosophy', he discussed the difference between instinct and intellect and condemned much of what he saw being taught in schools. Of course, adventuring, enjoying beauty and increasing understanding are religious activities, he argued. 'In reading astronomy or geometry, in making something, whether useful or otherwise, whether a milk jug or a flower garden, as beautiful as you can without violence in the former case to its efficiency, even small boat-sailing or Alpine climbing, you are convincing yourself of the Kingdom of Heaven as directly as mortal man can seek it: You are convincing yourself of the existence of God and the immortality of the soul, if you are at all capable of conviction.'

Having built *Triolet* in his early years at Christchurch, Green began his second boat for his own use in 1921. In this he was helped by a Douglas Harrison (no relation to Harrison the foreman) who used to come as a short-term wood-working pupil during his summer holiday. A meteorologist by profession, Harrison was a highly competent mathematician and the first to take seriously Green's method of yacht designing from solid equations. Harrison built a large sailing model; which was so fast and true on course with her self-steering gears, that the two men could scarcely keep pace in the sharpie Green had made for fast rowing.

It was on this same geometric principle that Green built *Bonny Betsy*, over three years. She was finished in the summer of 1924, soon after which Green and Bertha set sail for a twenty-three day cruise with Fanny, the dog. *Bonny Betsy* had a lifting sail and, in order to expose more canvas to a following wind, Green replaced the two small sails with one large one for 'inside work', although he always carried the small sails for use in heavy weather. It isn't often that Green sinks to the kind of light-hearted doggerel which follows - he was generally serious about poetry - but these verses certainly communicate his enthusiasm as well as providing a useful technical description of *Bonny Betsy*:

> O, August nineteen twenty four,
>   Her gales were fresh and strong;
> Yet we have struck the lucky hour,
>   And sung a cheerful song.
>
> The Bonny Betsy, she's our ship,
>   She's so extremely small,
> We cursed the wandering lust, the whip
>   That drove us forth at all.
>
> 'Tis sixteen foot she is by six
>   But though she is not big
> She has some most ingenious tricks
>   And a strange but useful rig.
>
> No mainsail but a mizzen she,
>   Foresail and jib, their size
> Co-equal, and their number three,
>   Or two or one, she flies.
>
> Her tiller has the craftiest stop:
>   And proud indeed I am
> That I can tow my cabin top,
>   And sleep under my pram.

By chance they met on this trip William Curtis Green and his family, who were coming out from Hurst Point in their 12-ton cutter, *North Star*. This was Bertha's first meeting with William's children and Green's first for many years. He hadn't for example, seen Joan - later to become such a good friend - and now 16, since she was two years old. Because they were still unmarried in 1924, Green and Bertha were neither inclined, nor invited, to board *North Star*, but confined themselves to what Green carefully describes as 'mutually respectful salutations at close quarters.' William subsequently wrote to say he couldn't imagine how his brother did such cruising in such a boat. Later he came down to Christchurch and enjoyably joined them on board to find out.

This was the first of many such cruises and Bertha was his usual companion. She loved it, although she had no experience of sailing before she met Green and was a life-long non-swimmer. On one occasion they spent a fortnight exploring the glories of Poole Harbour from Studland to Wareham.

> The dunes by day, the lonely lake,
>   The heather and the lark:
> By night the choiring wildfowl make
>   How musical the dark.
>
> How fine our supper table then,
>   How good before the night
> Our deeply cushion'd vaulted den
>   And our books by candle light . . .

begins a long poem celebrating such trips. He often wrote poetry during cruises, although he records that much of the above was written during a train journey.

Sometimes Green sailed with Macnamara and with friends from London such as Barbara Low and Henry Meulen. Green remembered one occasion when he went out in *Bonny Betsy* with Meulen, Meulen's daughter, Paula, and a 'nice young German.' When Bertha's hat blew into the water the German gallantly dived in fully dressed to retrieve it for her.

Henry Golding, Green's old friend and sailing partner from Strand-on-the-Green, visited and they sailed together in *Bonny Betsy*. They intended to take part in a Sailing Club race from Mudeford but, because of a rather strong south westerly wind, the club committee called it off. Breakers in the shallows and in the narrow channel of Christchurch Harbour were the problem and there was a risk of getting smashed up on foam covered sandbanks. Green and Golding went out anyway to show (off?) their mettle. *Bonny Betsy* performed so well that, in the end, Green and Golding sailed in and out of the harbour mouth several times just for the fun of it.

But as the 1920s wore on Bertha's health began seriously to decline. Her attacks of cardiac asthma became more frequent and it was clear that she and Green would have to change gear. *Bonny Betsy*, for example, was sold. He had neither the money nor the wish for a recreation she couldn't share. Money, moreover, was short again now that Green was without an income from teaching and workshop orders were falling off because of the Depression. It must have been quite hard for Green to face the new decade with optimism and equanimity.

Arthur Romney Green aged about 50

Chapter 9: The Troubled 1930s

Orders don't flood into woodwork shops during a slump and, by the beginning of the 1930s, even Green's reduced work force was under-employed. When an item of furniture made in the workshop was awarded a prize in a local competition, Green went to Bournemouth by bus for the presentation and came back with a silver trophy under his arm saying to the men 'I'd much rather have brought you some work than this thing.'

Nonetheless they did keep going. The Rural Industries Bureau (RIB) was a semi-government organisation whose purpose was to keep alive the traditional crafts of the English countryside. RIB sent some of Green's work to exhibitions which it held at Royal Agricultural Shows and this helped with sales and orders.

In 1931, at the 15th Exhibition of the Arts and Crafts Exhibition Society at The Royal Academy, Burlington House, Green had eight items on display. Nearly all were designed by Green and executed by his foreman William Merritt. The most expensive was a draw table in laurel whose price was £50-0-0 and the most modest was an arm chair in English walnut at 8 guineas.

It was also in 1931 that Philip Mairet gave Green a one-man show at The New Handworkers Gallery, 14 Percy Street, London W1. In connection with this exhibition Mairet also arranged for Green to deliver a lecture, with slides, to the Design and Industries Association, for which there was an admission charge. Green, swimming against the 'establishment' tide as usual, used this opportunity to accuse manufacturers of trying to manipulate taste. They were insisting, Green argued, that householders don't want 'dust traps' - so banal, ugly, mass-produced furniture is what they must have.

George Marston heard the lecture and drew the attention of his 'boss', R.I. Brooke, Director of the Rural Industries Bureau (RIB), to Green's talents and views. Brooke offered Green the post of Supervisor of Woodworking Shops for the Unemployed in the Distressed Areas of England and Wales. It would involve travelling to visit centres all over the country. And Brooke must have wanted Green quite badly for the post because the Bureau generously offered to fund a return fare home each week, however far away Green might be. This meant that he would be able to spend every weekend in Christchurch.

Examples of furniture made in the workshop. Above: an arm chair in chestnut. Below: dressing table mirror in English walnut.

While Green was reluctant to leave Bertha, now diagnosed as being seriously ill, for five days out of seven each week, he felt that because of her illness he couldn't really refuse any offer of paid work. There were doctors' bills to pay, medicines to buy and he wanted to make Bertha as comfortable as he could.

Money was very short, in spite of the usual help from William. And Green's bank had just intimated that he had exceeded his overdraft limit which was fixed at half the value of his property - whose title deeds were held by the bank.

Such work as there was could be done in the workshop as usual. After all, the business had run itself very well during all the years in which Green had also worked as a teacher. The men were used to the concept of an absentee gaffer. They were to produce five items for the 16th exhibition of the Arts and Crafts Exhibitions Society event held in 1935 at Dorland House, Lower Regent Street, including a walnut filing cabinet designed by Green and made by Merritt - although this was the last time Green was to exhibit at The Arts and Crafts Exhibition Society. Green accepted the RIB job.

Mrs Keynes came in for three hours each morning to help Bertha and there was also a live-in maid named Vera. With the lads working downstairs, the invalid Bertha was never actually alone, although Green always feared that she would suffer a bad 'attack' while he was away.

Graham Castle remembers clearly how the men used to take Bertha, politely and properly addressed as 'Mrs Green', cups of tea in bed when she wasn't well enough to get up. They took turns to take Fanny out for walks too.

But the advantage of their weekly separation was that Green and Bertha wrote to each other every day so, he reports happily, he acquired many delightful love letters from Bertha which he wouldn't otherwise have had.

One of the first things Green did as soon as he knew there would be money coming in again was to set Edgar Castle to build a 'pretty little sharpie'. It was about 16 foot long and 3 foot 6 inches wide, with sides in half-inch African mahogany and a masonite bottom. She was very light and handy and Green was able to moor her on the river bank just a hundred yards along the creek from the bottom of the garden of the property, now renumbered as 3 Bridge Street.

For about another four or five years Bertha, on good days, was just able to walk slowly and in stages along to the boat. Green fitted a comfortable seat into the boat for Bertha. Equipped with oars, a dagger board, a bamboo mast and one of *Bonny Betsy's* sails cut down, the sharpie was ideal for short trips at weekends, with the faithful Fanny always on board. Green taught Vera to row too so that she could take Bertha out on warm days in his absence. He thought the three of them looked very attractive in the boat: Bertha, always charmingly dressed, the bright complexioned, pretty Vera, and the dark-eyed, black-nosed Fanny.

Boat building in the workshop.

Green meanwhile - he was 60 in February 1932 - began each week by walking, early on a Monday morning, a mile to Christchurch Station, with heavy baggage, to catch the 8.00 am train to London. He would enjoy a leisurely breakfast in the train as it sped past the glories of the New Forest. He loved watching the crisp winter Hampshire dawns. Two or three hours would be spent in London, usually making designs for use in the occupational centres for the unemployed which he was going to visit that week. Then he would set off in the afternoon for, say, Newcastle where he would give six different half-day demonstrations on Tuesday,

Wednesday and Thursday before returning to London to write reports. Then it would be home to Christchurch on Friday evening.

The object of all this was to impart skill-training to unemployed men. Green, like Marston and Brooke, detested palliative solutions to social problems. He was scathing of those who wanted to treat effects to the exclusion of tackling causes. Giving clothing or food to the poor doesn't solve the problem, he argued. Trying to change the system which allowed them to become poor does. He believed that, in working with unemployed men to develop 'marketable' skills, he was, in a small way, helping to attack the cause of their distress.

For Christmas 1932 Green sent his foreman, William Merritt, the following poem. There is evidence that as he sent it to Merritt he probably sent copies to other friends that Christmas. Although it certainly isn't one of Green's finer poetic achievements, it neatly sums up his thoughts at the time of the slump:

> A few poor toys and cards we'll have
>   For children, sweethearts, wives
> And so above its open grave
>   Our wretched trade 'revives.'
>
> But still the miserable void
>   Is murmuring at our door
> Of those who must be 'unemployed,'
>   Because we're all so poor.
>
> And still - or so it seems to me -
>   The Herald Angels sing
> That Work's the cure for Poverty
>   O Angels, tell the king!
>
> Meanwhile by heaven's eternal laws,
>   We seek an alms for such:
> Alas, we're all too poor, because
>   We have produced too much.

Green was supposed to teach the unemployed men in the centres a bit about design, but he found that it was even more important that his 'pupils' should first learn something about construction. He showed them how to sharpen their poor quality tools and he taught them some honest joinery - which flew in the face of the prevalent 'braiding of machine-pressed bearings all over horrible little - or big - pieces of furniture, otherwise constructed of deal and plywood nailed together,

95

packing case fashion, the whole stained chocolate brown and heavily polished as if it were treacle.'

So, if they wanted decoration, Green set out to teach them how to cut simple mouldings or patterns with ordinary carpenter's chisels or gouges in the traditional way. He made some simple, but pretty, designs and circulated them. And he carried with him an immaculate piece of dovetailed woodwork - a wooden suitcase which contained actual models of the smaller pieces.

He earned the respect of the men he was teaching because he was unpretentious and unpatronising. He took off his jacket and handled the tools like one of them. By adopting the role of a practical instructor he soon stopped being a 'gentleman' adviser. He was pleased enough to record that when he attended a big conference in the Midlands, he was hailed by the delegates with friendly greetings such as 'Here comes the man who practises what he preaches.' He enjoyed the company of many 'bottom dogs' he met and worked with, although he commented that most people treat their dogs better than society treated most of these unemployed men. He liked most of the Advisory Officers who controlled the RIB areas too.

Chest of drawers made by Arthur Romney Green.

He also enjoyed the travelling. Only once since his return from Durban in 1900 had he been to the north of England (by bicycle in 1908, accompanied part of the time by Pleming). Yet he now found himself continually traversing the country. To begin with his work took him from Exeter to Newcastle, and from Grantham to the Rhondda Valley. Later he worked mainly in the Midlands, centred on Birmingham.

The new sights and novel experiences thrilled him. At Durham he went for a row in a skiff once his day's work was complete, at Lincoln he hired a bicycle and pedalled some miles along the canal to watch barges and at Nottingham he found some lovely barges only five minutes away from his hotel. He liked the primroses and cowslips he saw from train windows . . and trees, birds and buildings. He was ever a man thoughtfully to marvel at what he found.

He liked the novelty of hotel life too, having never been able to afford to use such places on his own account. He always had his drawing board with him and spent his hotel evenings in working out geometrical designs, thus also getting a lot of his 'own work' done. He also wrote, as always, and of course, he read. He particularly liked 'The Bull' at Blackburn, 'The Castle Inn' at Durham, 'The Nelson' at Liverpool, 'The Leopard' at Burslem and 'The Swan' at Chesterfield. His weekly expense account was in the region of £11.

Green described his two years in the distressed areas as 'a black nightmare streaked with silver and gold.' He detested some of the inhumane attitudes and rules he discovered in the under-funded RIB system.

Men attached to the workshops were not, for example, permitted to sell or receive money for their work. They could undertake only voluntary work or make items for their own use in order to remain eligible for the stigma-laden 'dole'. Materials were provided by the centres for charity work, but if a man was engaged on making something for his own household he had to buy the wood for it out of his meagre dole money. And, in order to learn, every individual had to be making something. Green observed that this meant that the men were so under-fed that fainting in the workshop - before the midday meal - was quite common, because fathers tended to give their children for breakfast what little food they had at home.

How bitterly Green recalled an interesting man he met at Grantham. The man was missing from the centre when Green enquired after him on a return visit. 'O he's in sad trouble, poor fellow,' Green was told. 'He took

2/6d (12p) for doing a job of gardening so lost his benefit and he and his family are well nigh starving.'

The town clerk of Chesterfield told Green, to the latter's horror and anger, that even if an unemployed miner was offered work, he was usually so malnourished that he was immediately sacked again because physically he couldn't manage the work.

Green believed the country's shortage of money was an entirely 'artificial' problem, considering that at the same time British banks were lending millions to Germany. The money was, he argued, financing the re-armament of Germany. Because those arms were then turned against Britain in 1939 the policy effectively meant that the British working man suffered twice.

Going to see the Unemployed

How fine the express at seventy miles per hour
And this swift rural loveliness to scan!
Heaven is without, and of the superman,
In this luxurious speed and sense of power,
Foretastes within, although the taste is sour.
For wither bound, O soldier of the van,
To what dark streets and haunts of Caliban
What filthy roots of this high-vaulting flower?

By their royal road, and rich hotels whereat
Their masters gorge, we come, how good and wise,
To slaves half starved whose masters dock supplies,
'Restrict production' as they call its - fat
Head and hard hearts ! But there the wreckage lies,
Not in the foreground: we have seen to that.

Green enjoyed the work for a while and was pleased that the salary enabled him to give Bertha two holidays. He was very conscious of how dull her invalid life must seem compared to his.

First he hired a car with a driver and installed her in a 'decent' boarding house at Barton-on-Sea. It overlooked The Solent where they had enjoyed so many sailing trips. She stayed there for ten days and he spent two weekends with her. It was a reasonably successful idea, although she did intimate that really, if she was to be on her own, she was happier in her own home.

Then later, during annual leave from the RIB job, he took Bertha for a lovely holiday at Windermere with Stanley and Emily Davies. They had been several times to Christchurch, but the Greens had managed only one return visit because the cost of fares was usually beyond their means. Green wanted Bertha to enjoy the luxury of a good long train journey, with nice meals in the dining car, as he had been experiencing, but was afraid that the travelling might prove too much for her.

He got around this by breaking the journey at Reading and spending two nights at the home of an old school friend, Ted Rowland, now a doctor, who drove them around the lovely Berkshire countryside on the intervening day. Then he and Bertha continued northward and spent a fortnight with Davies and Emily. Davies drove them round the Lake District and he and Green enjoyed some time on the lake in Davies's sharpie.

Back to work, the problem with the distressed areas job was that it was impossible for one man to do it properly. Sometimes a workshop had to wait six months between visits. Although Green was pleasantly surprised how much can be taught and learned in a few hours - then retained and applied for the months to come - the arrangement was clearly not satisfactory.

And it became more difficult still when the RIB committee, in controlling exactly where Green went and when, took to planning his itinerary so badly that he found himself spending more time travelling than teaching.

So they allowed him two assistants. One was Graham Castle, who went - with his new wife, a Christchurch girl named Mabel Forth - to the Midlands 'on loan' to the RIB and stayed for six years until the outbreak of war in 1939. The other was a man whom Green met at the Gainsborough Centre and trained for three weeks in his own workshop back in Christchurch. Green regarded them both as fine instructors.

Then Brooke, who had championed Green in his work, died suddenly in 1934 and, although Marston eventually took over as director, the mood changed. The committee - mostly those whom Green dismissively describes as 'fashionable West End ladies and gentlemen with Mayfair modernist ideas of the sort of furniture the unemployed should make for their homes' - refused to accept Green as a member. Most of them frankly disliked him. Without committee membership he had no control over his movements and felt this made the job impossible. Marston begged the committee members to change their minds but they were adamant.

Reluctantly, Green resigned the post and stopped this work at the end of 1934. He knew that no successor was to be appointed to follow him and he felt that he had let down his many friends amongst the 'bottom dogs'. If he had been a wealthy man, and had his wife had been fit enough to accompany him, he would have liked to continue to visit these workshops on his own account. As it was he had no choice but to abandon them.

During this period of employment with RIB Green published a series of articles, starting from Summer 1933, in its quarterly journal, *Rural Industries*. With the series title 'Woodwork for Unemployed Workers', these were what would now be jargonistically called 'how-to' pieces on subjects such as 'How to make a table,' 'Dovetailing, chairs, drawers, etc.', 'Some simple decoration and a good chair,' 'Hat pegs and other spiral designs' and 'Some principles of design'. They were illustrated with familiar photographs of items produced in Green's Christchurch workshop and with his usual mathematical design patterns. They were, presumably, written for the information of instructors in the regions.

Once back in Christchurch, Green's writing took other directions. From about the time he parted from RIB until his death, he made a number of contributions to *Contemporary Review* and became a regular contributor to *New English Weekly*.

Green described *New English Weekly* as a 'reforming journal'. He respected its enlightened approach to agricultural as well as to financial reform, along with its informed handling of foreign affairs.

Green wrote regularly for *New English Weekly* for the last ten years of his life on topics such as 'The Wrong Ends of Two Sticks: education and war' (4th June 1936) and 'Tomorrow's Education' (19th June 1937). He ranged across education, economics, politics, religion, craft and anything else which occurred to him or attracted his interest in his usual eclectic way - and with cheerful disregard for the customary artificial divisions which normally separate these areas.

In September 1937 Green lectured to the Economic Reform Club in London. In his talk, entitled 'Tomorrow's Art and Recreation', he argued that in an ideal society a man should be really enfranchised - free to choose his own work, just as he is to choose his wife or religion. Mairet chaired the meeting at which the lecture was given and it was later published by Vanguard Press as a pamphlet, priced one shilling.

Some of his writing flowed from his brief return to teaching upon resigning the RIB job. While Green was still working for RIB, T.F. Coade, headmaster of Bryanston - the independent boys' school founded near

Other items made by Arthur Romney Green.

Blandford in Dorset in 1928 to break the mould of a traditional public school - had attempted to 'head-hunt' him. It seems that Green was still remembered for his innovative teaching expertise locally in Hampshire and Dorset and that Coade had heard of him.

The offer was that Green should be the permanent Head Mathematical Master and that he should also have control of the woodworking shop. Having long felt that these two departments should be co-ordinated in schools, Green was tempted. The 'package' generously included every Wednesday afternoon with an overnight stay at home, as well as weekends off, with travel expenses paid to enable Green to spend as much time with Bertha in Christchurch, as possible. However, because at the time he was still anxious to continue with his work in the distressed areas, and not realising that this work would not last, he turned down Coade's offer.

When it became clear that his work in the areas was not likely to be permanent, Green contacted Coade and suggested that he might teach at Bryanston for a term on trial. This he did during the spring of 1935 and continued on trial during the summer term. Coade admired Green's work and often brought visitors to see him teach.

Green however, was now 63 and most of Bryanston's staff were very young. In a curious reversal of the usual 'generation gap' problem you find in most in staff or common rooms, Green, who was decades older than most of his colleagues, found them set in their ways, complacent and lacking in any kind of spirit. 'Intellectually speaking,' he wrote in a *New English Weekly* article - without naming the school - 'the interests and ambitions of the boys and masters were practically nil.'

Nonetheless, he would have quite liked the security and salary of a job at Bryanston on a permanent basis. Alas, a young master had been holding the head of department post in an acting capacity and was confirmed in it at the end of the school year. Green didn't have too many regrets, although he would liked to have published his three-volume opus *Mathematics Made Interesting* and believed that it would probably have found a publisher had its author been Head of Mathematics at Bryanston.

It certainly seems a pity that *Mathematics Made Interesting* never saw the light of day because, from the manuscript copy of Volume 1, still in the possession of the family, it seems a cheerful, upbeat attempt to de-mystify a traditionally 'shrouded ' subject. Its chapter headings include 'See-saws', 'Walking, Running and Cycling', 'Questions from the Cricket Field', and 'Mirrors, Searchlights and Telescopes'. It's a clear attempt to put the maths into the sorts of contexts likely to be of interest to the pupils

- actually still regarded as quite a 'progressive' idea. And its suggestions such as 'You should always try to understand what you are doing rather than to learn methods and formulae by heart. Certain things have eventually to be remembered but the greater the number of things you really understand the easier it will be to remember the whole lot, just as it is easier to remember a single picture than the separate piece of a jig-saw puzzle,' sound both extraordinarily modern and eminently sensible.

The book also gives a real sense of what it must have been like to have been a pupil in one of Green's mathematics classes. He clearly did turn himself into a talented teacher. He wrote other text books too, such as *Introduction to Analytical Geometry Pure and Applied*, but none of them was ever published.

Green was human enough to be pleased when one of the young masters at Bryanston, told by a pupil after he had left, that Green made maths interesting in his lessons, visited Christchurch several times to find out more about his methods. Green also enjoyed the fact that the young man who actually got the job as Head of Mathematics at Bryanston in 1935, later attended some lectures which Green gave to the Mathematical Association.

Back at 3 Bridge Street, now dubbed 'Woodcarvers' Hall' by the locals, John Champ, then just a few weeks past his fourteenth birthday, had begun in the workshop as the new apprentice on 1st January. He lived at Guss Cottages, near Guss Common on Roeshot Hill - since demolished. One of the first jobs he remembers working on - with another lad named Bob Smith, a student whose parents were paying fees for him to be there - was a boat called *Murlach*. Fitted with a 10-12 hp Morris Cadet engine, she was 23 foot long with two berths and made of 5/8 teak with oak ribs, like a Norwegian boat. She was sold to an Irishman.

By the summer of 1935, Green was settled back at Christchurch with the ailing Bertha. Alexander 'Sandy' Scott, whose parents had become good friends and customers, can remember having tea with Bertha in the bedroom above the workshop when Bertha was confined to bed. 'She had rosy cheeks, sunken eyes and white hair,' he recalls. 'She looked nice, but I got the impression she was very ill.'

Sandy Scott, 16, actually joined the workshop in 1936, travelling daily on a motorbike from his parents' home near Fordingbridge. He was, in his own words, 'a very backward boy' whose parents were desperate to find something he could do, or some way of remedying his educational

Murlach being built at Christchurch

difficulties. Green records that Sandy Scott read and wrote like a nine-year old when he first took him on. Green, assisted by Edgar Castle, taught him boat building and the mathematics needed for that. As well as boat building Sandy made bed ends for his parents, a book case in oak and a chest of drawers: 'every bit by hand' he says proudly. Several of these pieces are still with the Scott family.

Green and Edgar Castle restored Sandy's self-esteem and turned him into a fine boat builder with the ability to earn a living - and incidentally they taught him to read properly. Like John Champ, he has clear memories of building *Murlach*. Sandy Scott also made a 17-foot sharpie in mahogany, oak and pine in Green's yard - and he has her still.

Green brought in someone Sandy describes as a 'secretary' to teach him accounts and writing. Although he doesn't name him, Green records that Sandy Scott's experience is yet another example of conventional education just not bringing out the best in individuals. Sandy Scott, in turn, believes that he owes a huge debt of gratitude to Green, whom he describes simply as 'a great man.'

Workshop life continued as usual, with Merritt augmenting his income by teaching handicrafts at college. John Champ remembers that they used 'an old circular saw with a pedal that operated a chain and bandsaw, but beyond that it was all hand tools.'

Most of the timber - chestnut, yew, walnut, oak and occasionally mahogany - came from Lights in Fairmile. Green or Merritt would select it at the yard while it was still in tree trunks, then Lights would saw it into rough planks. John Champ, as the apprentice, then had to go and haul it through the streets of Christchurch on a noisy flatbed trolley with iron wheels.

Green, meanwhile, spent more and more time writing according to John Champ. Merritt and the others would get on with the making while Green sat at his big desk upstairs. Given the enormous output of articles Green was achieving at this time, and the size of *Work and Play*, the unpublished autobiography, it certainly must have been the case that he spent a lot of time on 'literary work', although he also travelled to meet other craftsmen and welcomed them to his workshop.

Kenneth Bowers, for instance, now aged 83, trained at Loughborough College in 1935-37 under Peter Waals. He was then invited to spend a few months at the workshop of Peter Waals at Chalford in Oxfordshire. Waals, who died late in 1937, had been foreman to the famous Ernest Gimson and was still constructing to Gimson's designs as well as his own.

Kenneth Bowers remembers meeting Green more than once at Chalford: 'A most charming chap who impressed us with his dedication to his craft. He was very interested in both my work and that of others from whom he took inspiration . . . It must have been sheer joy to be one of his pupils.' Kenneth Bowers also visited Green at Christchurch.

Green was by now an old man, although remarkably fit and active for one who had suffered from chest problems all his life and who still, in John Champ's words, smoked a pipe continuously - 'like a bloody steam train he was.' His wife was very ill. Very little money was coming in. And, as Viscount Grey had famously remarked in 1914, the lamps were, once more, beginning to go out all over Europe. Difficult times lay ahead.

Sailing *Murlach* in Christchurch Harbour

Above: in the workshop. Below: a boat made by A.R.G. in 1938.

Chapter 10: Bertha's Last Years

War against Germany was declared, for the second time in Green's life, on 3rd September 1939. He was 67 and Bertha 71. In the months leading up to this, and during the early years of the war, he had to divide his time between nursing Bertha as she needed more and more care, his ever more prolific 'literary work', managing a near-defunct workshop and trying somehow to make financial ends meet.

In the year or two before the nation was solemnly informed on radio by Prime Minister Neville Chamberlain that 'Britain is now at war with Germany', Green had written a series of incisive and far-sighted articles for *Christchurch Times*.

On 8th October 1938 Green used the previous week's Munich crisis as a shock tactic to draw readers' attention to the continuing plight of Britain's two million unemployed. 'We are all naturally relieved by the respite from war, although the continued activity of the ARP is not a very happy comment on our faith in the Anglo-German pact.' He went on to say that, 'There are not many people in the South of England who realise that there are those in the North and Midlands who would have welcomed a war on their own account, at any time during the last fifteen years . . . For then you see, whether as soldiers or munitions-workers they would have had more than 10d per day to spend on food and they would not have to dress in the ill-fitting second hand clothes of the charitable well-to-do.'

Two weeks later Green forthrightly discussed poverty in the age of plenty and announced a forthcoming public meeting in Christchurch at which Lord Northbourne, from Deal in Kent, was to be the speaker. William Curtis Green had been widowed in the early thirties. His second wife, whom he married in 1936, was Gwen, the dowager Lady Northbourne. The speaker at the Christchurch meeting on 31st October was Gwen's son and William's step-son. Green was never averse to making the most of his 'contacts' and argued that Lord Northbourne's landed gentry status would add to, rather than detract from, the impact of his enlightened views.

Several articles later, on 14th January 1939, the *Christchurch Times* was billing Green thus: 'A. Romney Green, our brilliant contributor and townsman, cannot today be dismissed with a mere mention; he is rapidly gaining a deserved popularity in National journals and magazines as a writer whose style is forceful and who pictures with his pen compassionate studies of our eager but workless workers. A mathematician and a deep student of our national (and international) monetary muddles, he is authoritative and provocative.'

How right they were about the national journals and magazines. *New English Weekly* had by now become one of his most regular outlets. On 10th October it published one of the pieces Green came to be proudest of. It was entitled 'How to win the war and how to pay for it' and argued, with detailed mathematics and graphs, for a form of negative income tax.

This was eventually reprinted as a booklet and, on the strength of it, in 1942 Green was honoured with a Fellowship of the Royal Economic Society. This gave him untold pleasure, not least - as he recorded gleefully - because it gave him equal status with Beveridge and Tawney, both by now very eminent men. Green, of course, was remembering how dismissive they had been of him forty years earlier at Haslemere, when he had known them both slightly.

In 1941 Green published a small anthology entitled *Wheat from the Waste*. It was an 'anthology of private and public utterances evoked by the Great Wars.' Included in it were extracts from letters and other writings from, or by, people Green knew - such as Trelawney Dayrell-Reed, Joan Yeo, Beatrice Dawkins, William Curtis Green and Edgar Castle, along with paragraphs written by Green himself, first published elsewhere, and quotations from Churchill, Bertrand Russell, G.K. Chesterton and the like.

For example, in *Wheat from the Waste* he quotes his friend Olaf Gleeson, a doctor from Southsea, who wrote to Green in a letter from London during the Blitz: ' . . . but most of all I love the loveliness of humanity these days. Conventions have broken down. One can entertain and be entertained freely. If you have no bed because your house has been bombed, half-a-dozen people are eager to take you in, not in spite of, but because of, the destruction, and one becomes human with no trouble whatsoever.'

Green published *Wheat from the Waste* privately from his own address, supplying it for 1s 3d (about 8p) post free on request. It was printed by Harrison, of 24 Bridge Street. He dedicated it to Bertha Green 'my wife and my best friend.'

At the same time, in the quiet of home, Green had been writing most of his long memoir *Work and Play*. He spent much of each day writing - often at a desk not far away from her - as Bertha was able to get up less and less often. John Champ remembers Green spent most of his time at his desk and was hardly ever in the workshop.

The workshop was quiet. Soon after war was declared, Edgar Castle went off to build boats, a reserved occupation - at first in Christchurch and later elsewhere. Sandy Scott, 21, was still working at 3 Bridge Street in 1940 and remembers some of the wounded troops from Dunkirk passing through the town. Then he went to Arnfields at Ringwood where he built dinghies and later to Bolsons at Poole to work on minesweepers. This now competent and employable young man, remember, was the lad who, only five years earlier, had been placed with Green as an almost 'hopeless case'.

William Merritt, after nearly two decades with Green, now went to work in a local aircraft factory. The restrictions on timber availability were such that it would have been very difficult to produce much woodwork even if Green had the manpower to do it. Graham Castle recalls that, during the war, the workshop was really just 'kept open' by an elderly man without much craftsmanship or aptitude.

Certainly there are no records of any quality items of furniture produced in the workshop after 1940. The few items traced made at 3 Bridge Street in the 1940s are relatively inferior - almost 'utilitarian', in fact. It is hardly surprising that, under such circumstances, Green seems to have lost much of his enthusiasm for the workshop in his last years - although there was always something going on there and he still took on apprentices and men who were invalided out of the services.

William Merritt in the workshop.

110

Mirror, carved by Samuel Dann, which was presented to John Champ.

Mairet came to stay with Green and Bertha in the summer of 1939 and thereafter fell into the habit of spending a week with them each summer. They enjoyed his company and got to know him very well. Eric Gill, with whom Green seems to have had less to do in the late 1930s, died in 1940.

Old friends Richard and Marie Mather dropped in when they could but, because they now lived at Saltburn, on the north-east coast near the Tees estuary, it wasn't very often. Marie Mather, much admired by Green because she came from country stock, sent Bertha lovely presents of scarves and shawls. Ruth Mather, Richard and Marie's daughter, twice came to stay at Christchurch for lessons in sailing and geometry - a tactful way for Mather to offer Green financial help.

In the late 1930s Richard Mather had ordered some furniture from Green for the home of his son, John Romney, who was about to marry. That furniture was eventually sold at auction by Tennants, of Leyburn in Yorkshire, after the death of Peggy, John's widow, in the early 1990s. It fetched less, perhaps, than it might have done, Kenneth Bowers comments, 'because, even now Green's name is less well known in the north of England than in the south.'

111

John Romney Mather, Green's godson and a fighter pilot, was shot down in the Battle of Britain over the Thames estuary on 25th August 1940. Mather had 'brought down' two German planes in five minutes and two more accompanied his fall. He left a young, childless widow to whom he'd been married for less than a year. In a tribute Green published this sonnet in *New English Weekly* on 23rd January 1941. He regarded it as one of his best:

Death of an Airman

Long-legged, long-armed, and iron-handed, plain
-looking and speaking, courteous and shy,
My namesake (little flatter'd you, or I
Yet slowly honouring each other's strain
Diverse) - what nerve, what power of hand and brain,
To ride that whirlwind Himalayan-high,
And single-handed so to shoot and fly,
To stoop and soar, to fly, to flight the plane

A hero amongst heroes greater far
Than all yet sung, victorious though in flame
You fell such heroes in so great a war
Are placed, as is so many a shining star
Amongst his peers: may this verse save your name
Out of so many who should be known to fame.

Percival Strong continued to be a much loved, regular visitor to 3 Bridge Street. William came frequently and so did Beatrice. Julia White was a customer who became a good friend in the late 1930s. A tall, strong woman, she farmed at Burley in the New Forest. She shared a number of Green's interests including literature. Once Bertha became too ill even to walk the few yards to the water's edge and to undertake short jaunts in boats, it was Julia who often drove over and went out sailing with Green. Unfortunately, once petrol was rationed she was able to come much less often.

Other good friends were Leslie and Elsie Goodwin, whom Green and Bertha had known for many years through the Bournemouth Poetry Society. The Goodwins lent Bertha a gramophone and some records of classical music, which she enjoyed once she had become effectively housebound and had been forced by failing health to give up weaving and her guitar. But most of the time Green and Bertha were on their own and he spent a lot of time reading to her - often from the English classics. Fanny, their old sheepdog, died in 1940, but they had, by then, acquired a black cat of which they both became fond.

Bertha needed medicine and her doctor, Dr Davidson, also recommended that she have a bottle of whisky per week. 'You've no idea how badly she needs it,' he told Green. Paying the doctor's bills and finding money for medication and whisky was now very difficult. Even William's largesse had dried up a little because, inevitably, his business too was affected by the war. At one point Green and Bertha were living entirely on the compensation that Green had received for a shed which had burned down in the garden.

They were saved by a legacy from Percival Strong, who died of cancer in the summer of 1941, to their great sadness. He had quietly and uncomplainingly become ill, but they had all three expected him to outlive Bertha. But, in the event he didn't and the money he left them helped Green through those penurious times. Useful cash gifts of money had also started to arrive each Christmas from Bertha's son Eric in far away Central America. Now a man in his fifties, Eric had finished paying for the education of his children and felt, apparently, that he could afford to be generous to his impoverished mother and step-father.

Before Bertha grew too ill to cope they took in boy boarders - lads who attended local schools and who needed somewhere to lodge - which brought in a little income, although Green seems to have found the presence of these 'young cormorants' somewhat exasperating. Green also generated a little income, as always, by teaching in the form of what we would now call 'private coaching'. In the early 1940s, for example, he made good use of the translation of Ovid he had produced more than 40 years earlier while he was in Natal, as the basis for some one-to-one teaching of Latin.

Inevitably Green had to undertake some 'nursing' of Bertha at times when those who came to help weren't there. He prepared her hot milk and biscuits, filled her hot water bottle or got her vacuum flask ready for the night. Although she hated him doing 'housemaid's work', and always struggled up to do it if she possibly could, he lovingly called it 'watering my flower'.

They continued to share the same bed, into which Green often crept late from his 'den', hours after Bertha was asleep. Their Great Occasions were able tenderly to continue - although at ever longer intervals - to within a few weeks of Bertha's death, provided he was gentle. His usual reverent attitude to sex persisted into old age.

He clearly had an ongoing need for sex, however, and for the company of attractive women, which never left him. Perhaps it was because of the growing infrequency of Great Occasions with Bertha that he came close to a little 'affair' with the district nurse, whose name was Madge. She came to 3 Bridge Street to nurse Bertha. Green fell into the habit of calling at her house in the evenings, ostensibly to discuss maths with Madge's husband. Bertha sensed this attraction and teased him about it. Madge began to give him 'dangerous' signals. Then, after setting up an assignation with Green, the nurse suddenly thought better of it and changed her mind. It was a near thing, but Green was forever glad afterwards that he hadn't succumbed and, in fact, remained totally faithful to Bertha until her death.

He habitually ate his breakfast and supper at a little table in the bedroom near Bertha and, at times when she was completely bed-ridden, his lunch too. He loved to watch her sitting, looking enchanting, in bed. He relished the sight of Bertha's white neck swathed in Marie Mather's shawl and the contrasting black fur of the affectionate cat when it jumped up to join her. At other times he left her to work at his workbench, at his typewriter or at a big drawing board.

In the spring of 1941, eighteen months before her death, they decided that it would be better for Bertha to be permanently downstairs so that she would be able to get out into the garden on good days. So the room which had previously been a showroom became a bed-sitting room. It was a big job to move the furniture out. Those who could get there - including William Merritt and Edgar Castle - came to help over a weekend. They had to take out all the banisters on the staircase and replace them afterwards.

The downstairs room was also slightly safer in air raids than a first floor room. Once or twice they heard the whistle of bombs nearby but, Green reasoned - with unconscious and poignant irony, given the way he was later to die - that he was more likely to be hit by a motor vehicle than to be killed by a German bomb.

In June 1941 Green and Bertha enjoyed their last holiday together. Mr and Mrs Scott, who lived at Godshill, near Fordingbridge, offered Green the use of a 'bungalow' in their grounds. Neither Sandy Scott nor his sister, Peggy, have any memory or knowledge of this and think that the building concerned must have been the school room in which they had had lessons as children. It offered a large comfortable space which Green and Bertha were able to use as a bed-sitting room. There she could sit in bed and enjoy the views of the New Forest while Green sat nearby writing. The Scotts collected Green and Bertha from Christchurch by car and sent them in a maid during their stay to wash up and to bring their lunch. Green characteristically observed that the maid was a 'charming

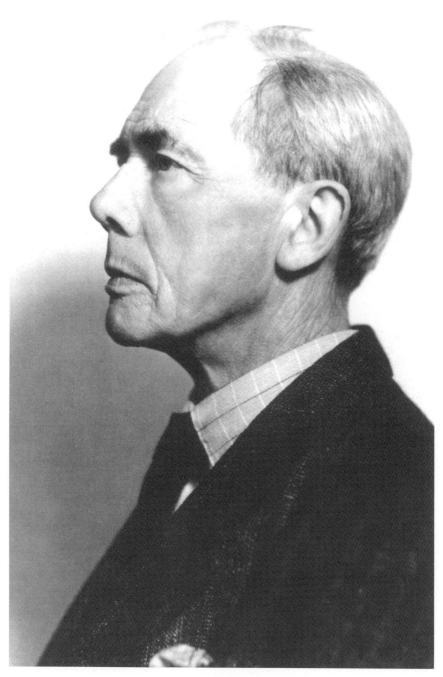

Arthur Romney Green.

fair-haired gypsy girl.' Green prepared breakfast and supper for the two of them and they enjoyed a peaceful interlude of privacy.

The idyll lasted just over two weeks. The weather was hot and sunny. Wild roses and other wild flowers blossomed in profusion. Although Bertha was by now too ill to travel beyond the building and its veranda, they were both very grateful for the hospitality of the tactful Scotts. Green thought the holiday was a 'thank you in kind' for what he had done for Sandy.

Although Bertha was very ill - and Green too with pleurisy - during the winter of 1941, and so weak on Christmas Eve that she wasn't expected to last through the night, she rallied and lived to enjoy one more summer. In March 1942 she was well enough to enjoy the cyclamens, primulas and daffodils, which he brought into her bedroom. In April she was strong enough to sit in the garden to see the pear and apple blossom, the irises and bluebells under the mulberry tree - and later the laburnum and roses. And, in between time, Green and Bertha read the *Forsyte Saga* together.

Mairet came to stay for a week in August and, for the first time, they discovered that he could recite Swinburn and Yeats beautifully, which gave Bertha great pleasure. Julia White, now farming in Berkshire, came two or three times. So did Olaf Gleeson, Sandy Scott and Mary de Latour. Visitors were good for Bertha if they were individuals she felt happy with.

But alas, she was growing palpably weaker and was soon no longer able to walk even to the summer house in the garden - so Green improvised a shelter from an old dinghy - ordered by Macnamara, but never paid for, years earlier - which he put nearer to the back door. There they could read and eat tea.

As the autumn drew on, and the sun grew lower in the sky, so Bertha's health took its final downward trajectory. She sat in the garden for the last time on Thursday 15th October. There followed a week of gradual sinking and ever longer periods of unconsciousness, during which Green hardly ever left her side, feeding her with a teaspoon and sitting inches away from her. Green was actually hanging over her as his 'lovely Bertha' peacefully ceased breathing and drifted into death on the morning of Friday 23rd October 1942.

Chapter 11: After Bertha

Beatrice came immediately. So did Julia White. Green was glad afterwards that these two women, of whom he was so fond, had this chance to spend a few days in each other's company because it led to their becoming friends. William Merritt and Sandy Scott were among the many people living locally who called to condole with Green.

Letters from loving friends and relations arrived in dozens. Clearly, as the letter from Green's younger sister, Margaret Curtis, makes clear everybody had been expecting Bertha's death for a very long time. 'So the blow has fallen at last after all these years of anxieties and hopes and fears and you will feel very lost, desolate with a gap that nothing can fill. .'

Philip Mairet wrote of Bertha that ' . . . even in her last illness [she] filled her presence with such beauty and love of the beautiful.' Stanley Davies's letter recalled the Greens' upstairs sitting room: 'That little room is a symbol, an ideal to me of simple, sound and good family fellowship, and at times of penetrating thought, real education and spiritual aspiration. I owe so much to you and also to her. Thank God for you both.' Edgar Castle, now far away at the naval dockyard in Bermuda, commented that 'Romney Green's' would never be the same again because ' . . . everything was centred around her; even the job which was awkward, getting a new piece up the stairs to show her was a pleasure.' And Trelawney Dayrell-Reed simply said 'You will have a lovely memory to live with.'

Bertha was buried in a quiet corner of the cemetery at Christchurch under a tree on Wednesday 28th October, 1942. She was 75. Green buried Bertha in Marie Mather's shawl and wearing in her hair a wooden comb which he had made himself. And of course the inscription on her gravestone is part of the poem:

> How should my heart not sing
> O Heart of gold
> In joy of thy perfection's manifold.

One wonders how Bertha actually spelt her middle name: Ann or Anne? It has an 'e' on her marriage certificate but not on her gravestone. On one occasion or the other Green, habitually rather casual about spelling, got it wrong. The double burial plot which Green bought cost him 3 guineas plus and extra 5 shillings for the registry of grant.

Bertha's grave in Christchurch Cemetery.

Now a widower in a country which had been at war for over three years, Green had to find some way of using his time. It must have been very hard indeed for him to adjust. For years he had devoted almost every spare minute to caring for Bertha. Without her, and with the workshop only a shadow of its pre-war self, there must have been a danger that time would hang heavy.

But Green was a resourceful man by nature. The first thing he seems to have done was to write the third part of his memoir *Work and Play*, describing in it his whole relationship with Bertha in candid detail from the first to last and using the writing as a transparent form of therapy. He even typed out and included many of the letters written to her by friends during her last years and her early letters to him, along with extracts from the many letters of condolence he received after her death. It's not very well written. It is simply the raw, but moving outpourings of a man beside himself with grief, who'd been in love for 44 years and who was now lost and lonely. Yet he never stopped rejoicing in his happiness and good luck in having Bertha to love, and to have been loved by, for so long.

He also continued to publish articles in *New English Weekly*. Amongst these was 'Something to look forward to' on 4th November 1943, 'Puzzles' a review of *Mathematical Recreations* by Maurice Kraitchik (Allen and Unwin) on 27th January 1943 and 'On Bellamy's Pre-history' on 20 April 1944.

His two part essay 'The Sailing Ship - the most wonderful invention of man' appeared on 26th October and 2nd November 1944 and was then published as a pamphlet, price 4d (less than 2p). He rarely confined himself to mechanics for long in his writing and usually soon moved from them to social reform and political thought. In this case he told the reader how sailing ships work - with diagrams - and then proceeded to debate the issues of war, peace, work and happiness. Only Green could argue in wartime - but beginning at this juncture to look ahead to the forthcoming peace - that ' . . . the revival of the sailing ship is the acid test for a sane and healthy social order; and what a solution it would be for the immediate and urgent problems of demobilisation especially of those younger and fiercer spirits who will turn in disgust and loathing from the sort of jobs which will be offered them, if jobs are offered at all, by our business-men committees of peace planners.'

Twice during 1944, once in May and again in November, Green gave broadcasts on the radio, presumably as a 'spin off' from published articles. For this he had to go to London, which he doesn't seem to have found any particular strain. Nor does he seem to have been in the least fazed by air-raids. On one occasion when he slept in London 24 bombs fell nearby during the night, but Green heard only twelve of them.

He would have liked to publish one or more volumes of his own poetry. At his death, amongst his papers was found the beginnings of such a collection. He had provisionally entitled it 'Poems of the Earth and Sea Volume 1.' In a loose-leaf scrapbook he had gathered many of his best published poems, and some typescripts of unpublished poems, and indexed them. He seems to have prepared this during the 27 months of his widowerhood. He also began work at this time on a long opus, unfinished in the event, entitled 'The Natural History of Art' - partly typed and partly in his inimitable, rather difficult to decipher, handwriting.

While Green scribbled and typed away at his desk the workshop barely ticked over in the hands of the very old and the very young. John Champ has kept a copy of a rather romantic magazine article about Green, but there's no indication of who wrote it, or of when or whether it was ever published. It must refer to the period after Bertha's death. The writer evidently knew Green's writings and claimed to be familiar with his work from public buildings, churches and homes. She, or he, mentioned having seen furniture in a house at Haslemere and described calling at 3 Bridge Street during the war.

He, or she, went into the workshop and was shown into Green's room at the back by a young man who told the writer that he'd been invalided out of the army. 'The little room seemed cramped with books and papers. An oil lamp was burning on the table and there was a kettle on the hearth, on either side of which sat Romney Green and a large black cat. Both rose to greet me. I liked that. I tried to see the features of this remarkable man, but in the dim light I realised only that he was pale and scholarly, bright, keen eyes and a merry smile. He spoke of poetry, ships and books . . .as a man who loves the lovely: the open sea or the countryside and honest creative work.'

Money was scarce. It was partly to help Green's finances that Sandy Scott moved in as a lodger after Bertha's death. Sandy had been ill with pneumonia in 1941, but was now back boatbuilding - this time at Banisters in Christchurch, so 3 Bridge Street was a convenient place to stay.

It was presumably while Sandy was at work that Green conducted what seems to have been his last little affair of the heart. He never lost his eye for a pretty girl or woman and now, much as he still missed her, without Bertha there he must have felt that there was no reason to hold back. His need for 'romantic' contact was as powerful as ever, it seems. Kitty Prout, nee Maidment, was a young married woman in her early twenties and Green was 72. Kitty worked in the dairy where Green went to buy milk and other groceries.

He fell 'in love' once more and took to writing poems and love letters to Kitty and leaving them for her on the counter. One thing led to another and before long Green and Kitty were meeting at 3 Bridge Street in the afternoons on early closing days when Kitty could get away from the dairy and during summer evenings while her husband, a builder named Ted, was playing golf.

Kitty is vague about precise dates, but this liaison would seem to have begun in the summer of 1944. 'He was a very good looking and very charming man and I was besotted with him,' she says. There seems to have been a lot of 'cuddling' and not much conversation, because Kitty found out very little about Green in her dealings with him, apart from the fact that 'he talked about all the famous poets and was very clever at maths.'

Interestingly, she recalls that the kitchen always smelled of fish, which would square up with Green's own recorded comment that after her death he found it a problem to find food for Bertha's rather indulged cat. Kitty remembers the mulberry tree too because Green sometimes gave her fruit to make jam.

Green also got to know Ted Prout because they could talk about building and construction together, although all knowledge of the clandestine meetings between him and Kitty was kept from Ted.

After Christmas 1944 Green was taken ill for several weeks, as so often before, with one of his recurrent bouts of bronchitis. Sandy Scott kept an eye on him and eventually Green recovered as usual.

On the afternoon of Monday 5th February 1945 Green went out by bicycle, probably to visit someone, or perhaps he went to the cemetery. It was the first time he had cycled out since his illness. At about 5pm - it was dark - he approached Barrack Road from Stour Road, where there were no traffic lights in those days. It was afterwards assumed that he was on his way home to change his clothes, since he had been expected at Ted and Kitty Prout's home that evening for a meal. Alas, he never got there.

Presumably because he was lost in his habitual absent-minded thought, Green cycled straight out of Stour Road without looking or stopping. He collided with a motor coach, which was travelling at less than 20 miles per hour. The coach driver swerved to avoid him, but the cyclist hit the body of the bus about half way along its length. Green fell and struck his head.

Local people still remember this accident. Captain Allen thinks, for example, that the 'motor coach' was a yellow Bournemouth Corporation bus. Green was a well known figure in the town, who cycled about in his rather old-fashioned green corduroy suit with its Norfolk trousers. His business, knee deep in woodshavings, had been a fixture in Bridge Street for 26 years. Children were wont to press their noses up against the window panes and marvel - or laugh. Regarded by many local people as an eccentric, distinctly Bohemian and 'a man with funny ideas' perhaps, but he was an integral part of the local scene. Everyone knew him. His accident would have been the talk of the town.

Green was taken by ambulance to Boscombe Hospital suffering from concussion. Someone from the workshop, Kitty doesn't know who it was, called on the Prouts to tell them what had happened to the visitor they were expecting.

According to Sandy Scott, who visited Green at the hospital three or four times, he never recovered consciousness. 'He just lay there white and still,' Sandy says. 'Sometimes I held his hand, but he didn't know I was there.'

Of course the family was informed and William came down to consult medical staff. A postcard from William to Sandy Scott, written on Sunday 11th February, six days after the accident, reads: 'I shall be grateful for a p.c. written on Tuesday with news of my brother's condition, if you can manage it. Please address it to me at The Athenaeum, Pall Mall, London SW1 Tel Whitehall 4843. The doctor thought continual visits to R.G. more harmful than otherwise so I am back here at the end of the telephone. Thanks for all your care. W. Curtis Green.'

Green died of cerebral haemorrhage, caused by concussion, on Wednesday 21st February, 16 days after his accident. He was 73, his birthday having fallen on 16th February during his period of unconsciousness.

He was buried with Bertha in Christchurch cemetery on Saturday 24th February. William was the chief mourner, although Sandy Scott and Mrs Leslie Goodwin were among the other local people. Perhaps because it was wartime and civilian travel was difficult, there doesn't seem to have been a major influx of friends and relations from further afield.

Green had designed a striking stone monument and kept it, half humorously for this moment. 'They're just waiting for me to go,' he used to joke with John Champ. A tapering obelisk about 5 foot high was to be added to the base stone and then topped with a, typically Green, truncated octahedron about 12 inches across. It has mathematical symbols incised on some of the faces. It is not known who carved this or when. Given Green's long friendship with Eric Gill it would be nice to think that perhaps Gill had done it for his old friend, but there is no evidence of this.

One of the patterns on A.R.G.'s memorial gravestone.

Arthur Romney Green's memorial gravestone.

Sadly, Green's innovative memorial has fallen prey to vandalism, an unimaginable problem when Green envisaged it. Its mounting is now damaged so that the solid geometrical 'ball' is loose and cannot be left precariously balanced because it could be dangerous. The crowning truncated octahedron is now kept locked away by the cemetery authorities, although they will reassemble it in situ for inspection and photographs if asked.

Something had to be done about 3 Bridge Street now that its owner was dead. It is rather sad to think that most of the furniture and equipment was simply sold off quite quickly and for low prices, although some pieces, Bertha's 'treasure box' for example, were kept by the family. Sandy Scott was asked by William and Beatrice to do much of this sorting out and to make arrangements. He bought Green's bandsaw himself, but sold it quite soon afterwards because he needed the money to buy an engagement ring for the girl he planned to marry.

Beatrice seems to have gone through the papers and personal things, probably with the help of her friend and cousin, Joan Yeo. William's daughter had become a good friend of Green and had agreed to be his literary executor. Even before her uncle's death Joan had been working with him on *A Craftsman's Anthology*. Because he respected her judgement, Green had acceded to many of her proposed cuts and, at her instigation, he had written a new introduction. Joan had also read and commented on much of *Work and Play* during the last year or two of Green's life.

Joan saved many of the papers which Green was working on at his death and, apart from some - those relating to the sale of the property for example - which seem to have been loaned and lost, these are still in family possession.

Someone found some colourful new love poems amongst Green's papers after his death. He had been writing poems to Kitty for some months but, always with one eye on later publication, he would certainly have kept copies of everything he wrote. It must have been these copies which were found. Someone, probably Beatrice - although it might have been Joan Yeo or possibly Julia White - worked out who they'd been written for, and took them to Kitty.

Kitty remembers that they were brought by a lady she didn't know who said 'I think these are yours.' Horrified, having carefully disposed of all Green's notes to her as they had arrived, Kitty told the person on her doorstep to take them away and destroy them. 'They were definitely not the sort of thing I'd have wanted my husband to have seen,' she says.

125

According to Graham Castle, he and Edgar toyed briefly with the idea of taking over 3 Bridge Street, as the war in Europe ended in May 1945, a little more than two months after Green's death. They believed that, managed in a single-minded way, the old workshop still had the potential to be profitable.

But it didn't happen. The premises were sold. Today 3 Bridge Street is a busy French restaurant and some of the inside layout is changed, although the main dining area is still exactly the same shape as it was when it housed six woodwork benches and the room was continuously filled with the scent of fresh cut wood. And the Dickensian oak bow windows, one of which Green's men replaced in 1925, still jut quaintly onto the pavement. Green's ghost isn't far away.

3 Bridge Street in modern times.

Chapter 12: Green's Lasting Contribution

So why is this obscure country woodworker worth finding out about more than half a century after his death? At the point when research for this book began few people had heard of him nationally, apart from the most serious students of 20th century English furniture, the readers of Eric Gill's letters and architecture buffs who knew vaguely that W. Curtis Green (d.1960) had had a brother. One hopes, however, that the mounting by friends, in 1997, of a blue plaque to commemorate Green's occupancy of 3 Bridge Street has re-awakened interest in Christchurch. Perhaps it will also intrigue visitors to the town enough to want to find out more about him. Even small pebbles can make big ripples.

If you measure success in crude terms of financial gain and prosperity, Green's life was an almost unmitigated disaster. He mostly lived from hand to mouth, 'fed by the ravens' as his daughter Beatrice so eloquently put it. He died almost penniless.

By leaving his first wife, Florence, at a time when such a course of action was totally unacceptable to almost all decent and respectable people, and certainly to those of the working middle and professional classes, he attracted widespread disapproval. He rendered himself *persona-non-grata* in many circles for many years. In seizing his own happiness, it could also be said that he caused untold suffering to Florence and to Harold Murray, to his own extended family and to Bertha's.

And yet Green's sincerity, lack of hypocrisy, intelligence, integrity, charismatic personality and sheer *joie-de-vivre* made it difficult - if not impossible - for those who knew him to remain vexed with him for long. Many of those who remember him, or who wrote their memories before they died, speak of Green almost hagiographically. A man who can, after all these years, inspire, or even compel, such devotion, is clearly worth getting to know.

Where he is known at all, Green is remembered as a furniture designer and maker. He's considered important enough, for example, as a 'descendant' of William Morris, disciple of Ruskin and maker in the Arts and Crafts tradition of Gimson and the Barnsleys, to be represented at the Victoria and Albert Museum, Britain's premier fine arts collection. The V & A has two items by Green, both bequeathed in 1982 by James Campbell Thomson of Godalming in Surrey. Thomson commissioned a large number of pieces from Green between 1924 and 1939. These included a dining room suite, a bedroom suite and a number of fine items for the living room.

The piece on display at the V & A is a collector's cabinet for photographs which stands four foot high, is not quite a yard in width and is 16 inches deep. It is made in walnut and Cuban mahogany inlaid with ebony and box. Its thirty small drawers have attractive two-tone stringing and the handles - typically for Green - are regular hexagons with three concentric circles on each one. The drawers are concealed by two doors with diamond panelling. It's a magnificent piece and stands proudly - but, because so little has hitherto been known about its maker, almost anonymously - in the same gallery as furniture by Morris, Gimson, Sidney Barnsley and others whose lives have long been well documented.

A second piece by Green - a rather heavy, but splendid, 56 inch high display cabinet in walnut inlaid with ebony from the same bequest, is also held by the V & A but, sadly, not on public display.

A whole display 'room' in the Red House Museum, Christchurch is based around a Green dining suite. Then there is a Green dining chair, made in walnut with an oak-framed seat, at Cheltenham Museum. It was given in 1978 by the executors of Stanley Davies who had died the year before. The design for this chair is held in the Green archive at Abbot Hall, a museum in Kendal, not far from where Davies lived and worked at Windermere for more than fifty years. Green described the back of curved lathes as a 'wheatsheaf'. The drawing gives detailed typed instructions on the mathematics of converting a straight wheatsheaf into a parabolic one and - as usual with Green - the curve of the seat and its gradient were also calculated mathematically.

Bert Wynn of Durham is a practising woodworker who finds Green's best work outstanding for 'the sheer quality and artistry of the design.' Having himself tried to make tables and chairs to Green's designs, he finds that 'the reason modern furniture makers cannot produce those things is that they can be executed only with hand tools. I think Green was easily the most gifted designer working in the period 1900-1940, although he goes largely unrecognised,' says Bert Wynn.

Examples of Arthur Romney Green's work.

And that's quite a claim since Ernest Gimson, Sidney and Edward Barnsley, all worked during that period. 'Green's workshop,' Bert Wynn continues, 'was capable of a much greater range of items than any other: sailing dinghies, draw leaf tables and extremely complex chairs, the most difficult of all furniture to make.'

But some of the 'ordinary' pieces which Green's workshop made for local artisan homes was, it must be said, pretty mediocre, especially during the last few years of Green's life. In spite of what Green's extant admirers and former workforce now claim about his never compromising on standards, there are pieces around with ply-wood backs, crudely pegged together and indifferently assembled. When they were making for the everyday local market, speed and affordability were presumably more important than perfection.

However, when Green's 'art' furniture comes up for sale it now fetches prices which would have astonished its designer - who sold many of his workaday items at under £10 and for whom a fifty-pound piece was something very special indeed. When Sotheby's sold off most of J.C. Thomson's Romney Green furniture in 1982, a walnut glazed display cabinet was expected to fetch £500-800 and a walnut occasional table £100-150.

By 1990 Christie's was offering a large oak sideboard by Green - a rather eccentric looking piece 10 foot high - at a predicted price of £3,000-£5,000. In the event the piece sold for £7,425 (£8,250 inclusive of the 10% buyer's premium). At the time of writing the Southampton Institute is negotiating to buy a quite plain Romney Green bookcase, for which the anticipated price is in the region of £2,500.

A man whose furniture is displayed in such august surroundings, and which, because it is now regarded by the *cognoscenti* as so interesting that it commands such prices, deserves to be better known as a personality and as a thinker - which is part of the rationale for this biography.

But only one part, as this book makes clear. Green only ever regarded woodwork as one strand in the richly woven tapestry of his full life. It was never the totality, and at times seemed to become almost a sideline while he engaged himself in other things. Poetry for example. Green was a fine poet, as many of the examples quoted here show. It is very regrettable that, apart from the few Green poems which were published in *A Craftsman's Anthology* (Allen and Unwin 1948), hardly any of his poetry has ever been published by a 'mainstream' publisher. And much of it, including several of the poems quoted in this book for example, was never published at all. In turn, that has meant that he has never been anthologised, so that he has yet to be read by a wider audience.

Of course, like all poets the quality of his work is uneven. Some of his verse is trite, some is arch, quite a lot of it is over-written and some is banal. Nonetheless the best of Green's verse, often evidently influenced by Tennyson and the earlier Romantics such as Keats, bears comparison with Gerald Manley Hopkins or Siegfried Sassoon. Green used poetry for everyday occurrences or events which triggered ideas, as a protest, as a descriptive written form, as a means of conveying enthusiasms and occasionally, jokes. Much of it is unapologetically autobiographical. He experimented with most of the standard poetic forms - sonnets, quatrains, blank verse, the traditional five-stanza iambic pentameter, beloved of Shakespeare and many others, and, from time to time, long Alexandrine or even fourteener lines.

Green should certainly be read today as a poet for 'Green Places', 'A Tryst' and 'A Strange Visit'. There are many other Green poems which would generously repay careful reading and study too. For instance, the immaculately articulated sense of joy and discovery in a sonnet such as 'The Sailing Ship' - with all its echoes of Blake - as Green finally worked out that he could use solid equations similar in kind to sailing ships of various types, make this a fine poem:

> This master-work of man - at last the key
>   To this elusive miracle I hold!
>   Follow to theirs far-flung harmony.
> No more, even Einstein, will I envy thee
>   Thy range of interstellar spaces could,
>   Thus to decipher here this wondrous mould
> Of beauty, power, and speed enough for me.
>
>   This mould of cross-wise plank and timber wrought
>   By wind and wave - unletter'd age-long thought
> And dauntless toil in conquest of the sea!
>   Well may I ask, And which most wonderful,
>   The elemental, means the perfect hull,
> The script of its obscure geometry?

And that, of course, also serves as a reminder of another of Green's loves which he described in himself as an 'obsession' - sailing and boats. From boyhood almost to death Green liked fewer things than to get out on the water. The boats he built - and he seems never to have sailed much in any vessel other than the ones he painstakingly designed and, usually, built for himself from first principles - and the journeys he made in them must surely speak to any sailor today?

At no point in his life could Green ever have afforded to buy a boat. So, in the early years, he made them. Later he had the men in the workshop to do some of the making, but Green always designed his own boats. And they were designed for speed and efficiency. Any boat builder and/or sailor is bound to find something in Green's 60 years of sailing to interest him or her - especially as some of Green's boat building techniques broke new ground.

There is something wonderfully simple, but also profoundly inspiring, in the peaceful - even when the weather was rough - picture of Green and Bertha sailing and adventuring along the South Coast on, say, *Bonny Betsy* in the 1920s, or earlier up and down the Thames from Strand-on-the-Green.

Of course Green was a prolific prose writer as well as poet. It is from the study of his prose writings that one can piece together so much of what he thought and believed. Yet his prose style is often turgid. He seems usually to have written much better within the self-imposed restraints of poetry. Much of *Work and Play* is really rather poorly written, with far too many long and rambling sentences. It's incoherently constructed, over punctuated and - oddly - not even very reliably spelled.

The articles in *New English Weekly*, and the many dozens Green had published elsewhere, are more incisive and tighter - probably because they were carefully edited by staff at the magazines and newspapers which published them.

Nonetheless, the content of Green's prose outpourings makes fascinating reading. Here was a man with firm, strongly-articulated, views - broadly speaking 'leftist', although his free-ranging ideas defy any kind of packaging label - about nearly everything. If you try to pin Green's views down to an ideology it's easier to say what he wasn't. He had, for example, no truck with Conservatism, but it would be far too simple to say that he was therefore a socialist. In fact, in his last years, he professed to loathe 'socialism' - by which he meant the everyday politics of the Parliamentary Labour Party. He was looking for more radical solutions to the 'social problem'. He half believed that communal ownership of all property and equal wages for all would solve the 'economic problem' - but it would be a gross over-simplification to say that these views meant that he was a Communist. He never maintained any affinity to any organised political group for long because he always quickly found himself disagreeing with other members on specific issues.

None of the fundamental problems Green agonised about have been solved, although some of the details have changed. We still have a high percentage of unemployed people in Britain. And one is somehow glad that Green didn't live to see heads of denationalised utility industries in receipt of six-figure salaries while thousands of 'bottom dogs' live in shop doorways, under sleeping bags and in cardboard boxes on the streets of our cities as the second millennium gives way to the third.

Politicians and other solution-seekers could do worse than to give serious consideration to what Green said and thought about these issues. Green went out, sleeves rolled up, literally as well as metaphorically, and worked amongst his 'bottom dogs'. He employed some of them in his workshops and therefore knew them as flesh-and-blood human beings. 'The poor' weren't just statistics - as they were for so many of the do-gooders whom he despised - just as he would their descendants still in positions of power today.

His attitude to education is refreshing too. 'Utilitarian' was one of his strongest perjoratives. He had high Romantic views about the power of art and beauty to captivate and enlighten the young. Yet he also wanted them to be taught practical skills which would enable them to make things which were useful as well as beautiful - always of course in an adventurous way. He didn't see beauty or science, or art and technology, as separate entities.

Today's curriculum designers, who have forgotten that the mind is 'a pile which simply requires kindling-wood to start the flame of original thought and ardour for truth' - because they are so intent on trying to fill it up like a vessel - would do well to consider Green's imaginative views. Just as he went out to the unemployed so Green clocked up many years in the classroom - the equivalent of nearly twenty full-time years of teaching if you add up all the bits and pieces he did here and there. He taught in a whole variety of different sorts of schools. He was no theoretician or 'educationist'. He knew from experience how children learn and what benefits them. He became a gifted teacher.

Then, of course, there was Green's personal life. One can feel great sympathy for poor deserted Florence. Her only 'crime' really was to be vivacious and flirtatious and to throw her hat at a man with whom she was incompatible. The child Beatrice, whose father disappeared from her life for all those years, must also have suffered. Nevertheless, one feels that because Green and Bertha loved each other with such lasting devotion they deserved their happy ending. Not that it was easy for them. Bertha, in particular, paid a high price for leaving Murray. Moreover her health was in decline almost from the time that she and Green first set up home together. And yet, like Mellors and Connie in *Lady Chatterley's Lover*, but unlike Vronsky and Anna in *Anna Karenina*, both books which Green and Bertha would have known well - fate treated them fairly kindly.

Green thought that he had enjoyed amazing luck in his life. He never stopped being thankful to the gods for letting him have Bertha. He knew too that it was the sheer eclecticism, and his continuous journey of discovery through life, like that of Tennyson's Ulysses, which had constantly brought him great satisfaction and happiness. He regarded over-specialisation as the vice of the ambitious man and argued that it was diversity of interest which had helped to make him a rounded and fulfilled person. There must be lessons in this for every generation.

Ornate Cabinet made by Arthur Romney Green.

134

Afterword on Sources

Romney Green was virgin biographical territory when I began this book. Nothing coherent, or researched from original sources has, it seems, previously been written about his life, work, loves and complex personality. In fact, even the little that was 'known' about Green is mostly wrong. Almost all the brief entries about him in reference books contain serious biographical inaccuracies - and that includes John Gloag's *English Furniture* (1934,1944 & 1948) and David Joel's *The Adventure of English Furniture* (1953), both highly-respected standard works. From somewhere, for example, has sprung an oft-repeated tale that Green was a brilliant mathematician and a Cambridge Wrangler - someone who achieves a First in all three parts of the mathematical Tripos - which plainly he wasn't. Then there's confusion about where Green was born, where and when he had workshops and whom he knew.

Even the catalogue to accompany a 1978 exhibition of W. Curtis Green's work, published by the family firm, is inaccurate on events in the childhoods of William Curtis and Romney Green. Inevitably the mistakes have been frequently repeated, and the myths perpetuated by various writers who have recycled them in other writing - and that, I'm afraid, includes me. I published one or two sadly error-laden magazine articles about Green - before the intrigue which researching those articles aroused in me led, eventually, to this book.

My job, then, as Green's first biographer, has been to set the record as straight as I can with the information at my disposal. And I've unravelled it by using primary source material almost exclusively. The most constantly useful of these has been Green's unpublished autobiography *Work and Play* - an ironic title since Green, of all men, didn't distinguish between his leisure and his labour. Both were just complementary parts of his full life. He wrote the bulk of it in the 1930s when Bertha was ill and then revised it after her death in 1942.

Three quarters of *Work and Play* is lodged in the National Art Library at the V & A Museum in London. The fourth part is missing, presumably destroyed in 1945 by Beatrice when she sorted out her father's effects after his death. She was evidently unhappy about some of what her father had written, having scribbled crossly - in rather childish and unformed handwriting - at the end of section 1: 'This is all imagination. He has no evidence (and neither have I) for making these statements.' The lost Part IV contained chapters entitled 'War Time', 'A Romantic Episode', 'The Promised Land' and 'Various Appendices'.

Different designs of chairs.

Work and Play is, in the words of Joan Yeo (later Joan Yeo-Marsh), Green's late niece and literary executor, a 'maddening work'. It is rambling, repetitive and unchronological. It contains dozens of lengthy digressions into Green's ideas for righting national and international wrongs. He thinks nothing of suddenly devoting 10 pages to some remembered debate with someone he'd admired, or disagreed with, or both. Because he was simultaneously absorbed in so many things, you sometimes feel that he doesn't tell the reader all that much about any of them. Various people - Joan Yeo-Marsh, Beatrice Dawkins and Gwen Curtis Green, William's second wife - attempted to edit the manuscript, which is annotated and with many sections crossed through, alongside Green's own hand-written amendments and comments. Many of his more frank and personal revelations have been heavily scored out, presumably by Beatrice. I suspect the 'editors' gave up in despair at trying to impose order on something so chaotic.

By his own admission Green didn't remember dates and time spans or attach much importance to them. I have therefore made extensive use of other material to supplement and to corroborate, dating incidents as accurately as I can wherever possible. Fred Green's letters, which Minnie Green later gathered together and typed up with a commentary so that each of her children could have a bound copy, were useful. Minnie Green wrote a detailed family memoir about the Curtis family home at Alton, also bound in a folder for the family. This, too, provided insights into Green's childhood. Both of these 'books' are still in family possession.

I have also used other writings by Green such as his poems, articles, transcripts of lectures and broadcasts, letters and drafts for text books, as well as tributes to, and comments made about Green, by others. Some of these are in the National Art Library. Others are held by the family. There is also a Romney Green archive at Abbot Hall in Kendal. Most of his published articles in magazines and journals, such as *New English Weekly*, *The Builder* and *Yachting Monthly* are accessible through the copyright libraries. Photographs too - and there are a surprising number of these in museum collections and in private hands - have their own stories to tell.

Fiona MacCarthy's splendid biographies of Eric Gill and of William Morris (both Faber & Faber, 1989 and 1994 respectively) have proved a valuable source of background information. I have also referred several times to *The London Encyclopedia* edited by Christopher Hibbert and Ben Wienreb (Macmillan 1983), to *Dictionary of National Biography* (OUP, various dates) and to *Good Citizen's Furniture* by Annette Carruthers and Mary Greensted (1994, Cheltenham Art Gallery and Museums in association with Lund Humphries).

At the time of writing there is still a small group of elderly people who remember Green in the 1920s, 30s and 40s at Christchurch and elsewhere. Their memories have often corroborated, explained - or occasionally refuted - what Green himself wrote. Each individual offers a unique 'angle' on Green's work and compelling personality.

Since I began writing - and advertised the fact - I have also been approached by various people: those who've inherited Green furniture through their families, who have some personal memory of him or who have encountered Green through academic study. I have used in my text almost everything which has emerged this way.

I have told Green's life story chronologically - which I don't suppose he would have cared for - diving into his multifarious interests and activities as and when they crop up. Artificial as this method is, it seems the only possible way to make his story flow comprehensibly. Sadly, it is almost certainly the eccentric 'wandering' quality of *Work and Play* which rendered it unpublishable.

Green often 'changed' names in his writing in order to disguise the identities of some of those who were then still alive, or whose close relatives were living. In *Work and Play* Percival Strong, for instance, is referred to as 'Large' and Harold Murray as 'Wallace'. He called Florence 'Dahlia' and concealed her family name of Garman. I have tracked down real names - through the Family Records Centre and from references elsewhere in the writings - and reverted to them for clarity. Green also played some rather transparent (and pointless?) Hardy-esque games with place names, calling Christchurch 'Riverchurch' and Bournemouth 'Seabourne'. I have used conventional place names throughout.

Except where a book is referred to very specifically and only once so I have dropped its title into the text, I have chosen not to clutter my pages with footnotes and continual tedious references, preferring to credit sources here in a more general way.

Susan Elkin, Kent, Autumn 1998.

Index

C

California. 37, 38, 82
Cambridge University. 11 et seq., 18, 26
Cannock Chase. 16
Carter, Frederick. 54
Castle, Edgar. 66, 72, 93, 105, 109, 110, 114, 117, 126
Castle, Graham. 23, 29, 63, 65, 66 et seq., 84, 85, 93, 99, 110, 126
Catherington Church, Hants. 70, 71
Chalford, Oxon. 105, 106
Champ, John. 103, 105, 106, 109, 111, 120, 123
Charterhouse, Surrey. 70
Chattock, Romer. 64, 65, 74
Cheltenham Museum. 128
Chesterfield. 97, 98
Chichester Harbour. 22
Christchurch, Dorset. 3, 8, 23, 29, 61 et seq., 80 et seq., 91 et seq.,
                     108 et seq., 117 et seq., 127 et seq., 138
Christ Church, W. Bromwich. 14
Christchurch Cemetery. 117, 121 et seq.
Christchurch Harbour. 89, 106
Christchurch Poetry Society. 80, 82
Christchurch Priory. 63, 74 et seq.
Christchurch Sailing Club. 70
Christchurch Times. 108
Cliffords Inn. 46
Coade, T.F. 100, 102
Cobden-Sanderson, T.J. 48
Collis, John Stewart. 27
Contemporary Review. 100
Comyns, Jack. 10
Cooper, Paul. 45
Cox, Mabel. 44, 47, 49
Cox, Oswald. 47, 49
Craftsman's Anthology, A. 82, 125, 131
Critchfield, Bosham. 22 et seq.
Curtis, Frederick. 48
Curtis, Margaret (nee Green). See Margaret Green
Curtis Museum, Alton. 7
Curtis, Dr William. 1

D

Dann, Samuel. 65, 111
Dartmouth. 10
Davies, Stanley Webb. 66 et seq., 73, 99, 117, 128
Dawkins, Beatrice (nee Green). See Beatrice Romney Green.

Dawkins, Rev. Vincent. 84
Dayrell-Reed, Trelawney. 77, 79 et seq., 109, 117
'Death of an Airman'. 112
Design & Industries Association. 91
Dilkes, Cicely. 22
Dillaway, D.D. 30
Ditchling, Sussex. 52, 62, 72
Durban. 15 et seq., 29, 31, 57, 77, 97
Durban Government High School. 15
Durham. 97

E
Eades, Alfred. 64, 65, 72
Economic Reform Club. 100
Edney, Leslie. 64, 65
Exeter. 8, 97
Exmouth. 7 et seq., 14
Eyres, Margaret. 80, 82

F
Fanny. 74, 78, 79 88, 93, 94, 112
Field. 26
Fry, Roger. 37, 57

G
Garland, The. 15
Garman, Florence. See Florence Emma Green.
Garman, Mary. 19
Garman, Walter. 16
Garman, Dr William Chancellor. 14, 15
Garrod, (Schoolmaster). 17, 21
Gill, Eric. 47, 52, 56 et seq., 61, 68, 70, 82 et seq., 111, 123, 127, 137
Gill, Mary. 57, 84
Gimson, Ernest. 30, 45, 51, 105, 128, 130
Gleeson, Olaf. 109, 116
'Going to see the Unemployed'. 98
Golding, Henry. 32, 89
Gooch, G.P. 12, 18, 24, 47
Goodwin, Elsie. 112, 122
Goodwin, Leslie. 112, 122
Grahamstown, S. Africa. 7
Grantham. 97
Great Barr, W. Bromwich. 14, 16, 29
Green, Beatrice Romney. 24 et seq., 32, 38, 42, 44, 79, 84, 85, 109, 112,
                                    117, 125, 127, 133, 135, 137

Netherton, Devon. 30
Newcastle. 94, 97
New English Weekly. 23, 52, 100, 102, 109, 112, 119, 132, 137
New Handworkers Gallery. 72, 91
Newton Abbot. 10
Newton College. 10, 14
National Guilds League (NGL). 57
Northbourne, Lady Gwen. See Gwen Curtis Green.
Northbourne, Lord. 108
Nubian, The. 7, 16

O
Oliphant, Alfred. 54
Oxford. 8

P
'Pacifism'. 58
Pearce, Joseph. 14
Pepler, Clare. 50 et seq.
Pepler, Douglas (later Hilary). 48, 50, 52, 73
Pike, Manning. 85
Pleming, Henry. 30, 31, 35, 50, 97
Poems. 31
Poole Harbour. 89
Prout, Kitty. 120 et seq.
Prout, Ted. 121, 122

Q
'Quaestio'. 81
Quakerism. 1, 5, 39, 48

R
Reiach, Herbert. 57
Red House Museum, Christchurch. 68, 128
Reddie, Dr Cecil. 60
'Reprieve'. 79, 85
Rothermere, Lord. 73
Royal Academy, Burlington House. 71, 91
Royal Economic Society. 109
Royal Institute of British Architects (RIBA). 31
Rural Industries. 100
Rural Industries Bureau (RIB). 91, 96, 97, 99, 100
Ruskin, John. 1, 19, 33, 66, 128
Russell, Bertrand. 33, 49, 57, 109

S

T

U
Unwin, Bernard. 30

V
Victoria and Albert Museum, The. 128, 135

W
Waals, Peter. 105
Walker Art Gallery, Liverpool. 71
Walker, Emery. 48
Wandsworth Common, London. 1 et seq.
Wedgwood, Lord Josiah Clement. 33
Wessex. 81
Wessex Review. 80, 81
West Bromwich Art School. 14
West Mersea, Essex. 60, 61, 63
Wheat from the Waste. 109
Where Men Decay. 33
White, Julia. 112, 116, 117, 125
Wimborne Grammar School, Dorset. 80
Windermere, Cumbria. 66, 99, 128
Woodwork in Principle and Practice. 61
Work and Play. 84, 105, 109, 119, 125, 132, 135, 137, 138
Wright, Richard B. 68
Wynn, Bert. 128, 130

Y
Yachting Monthly. 19, 57, 137
Yeo, Joan (nee Green and later Joan Yeo-Marsh). 26, 50, 72, 82, 88, 109, 125, 137